Essential Series

C000146977

Springer

London
Berlin
Heidelberg
New York
Barcelona
Hong Kong
Milan
Paris
Singapore
Tokyo

Also in this series:

John Cowell
Essential Visual Basic 5.0 *fast*
3-540-76148-9

Duncan Reed and Peter Thomas
Essential HTML *fast*
3-540-76199-3

John Hunt
Essential JavaBeans *fast*
1-85233-032-5

John Vince
Essential Virtual Reality *fast*
1-85233-012-0

John Cowell
Essential Visual J++ 6.0 *fast*
1-85233-013-9

John Cowell
Essential Java 2 *fast*
1-85233-071-6

John Cowell
Essential Visual Basic 6.0 *fast*
1-85233-071-6

Ian Chivers
Essential Visual C++ 6.0 *fast*
1-85233-170-4

John Vince
Essential Computer Animation *fast*
1-85233-141-0

Aladdin Ayesh
Essential Dynamic HTML *fast*
1-85233-626-9

David Thew
Essential Access 2000 *fast*
1-85233-295-6

Ian Palmer
Essential Java 3D *fast*
1-85233-394-4

Matthew Norman
Essential ColdFusion *fast*
1-85233-315-4

Ian Chivers
Essential Linux *fast*
1-85233-408-8

Fiaz Hussain
Essential Flash 5.0 *fast*
1-85233-451-7

John Vince
Essential Mathematics for
Computer Graphics *fast*
1-85233-380-4

John Cowell
Essential VB .NET *fast*
1-85233-591-2

Aladdin Ayesh
Essential UML *fast*
1-85233-413-4

Simon Stobart
Essential PHP *fast*
1-85233-578-5

Fiaz Hussain

Essential Dreamweaver® 4.0 *fast*

Rapid Web Development

Springer

Fiaz Hussain, BSc (Hons), MSc, PhD
University of Luton, Park Square
Bedfordshire LU1 3JU

Series Editor
John Cowell, BSc (Hons), MPhil, PhD
Department of Computer Science, De Montfort University, The Gateway,
Leicester LE1 9BH

British Library Cataloguing in Publication Data
Hussain, Fiaz, 1960–
    Essential Dreamweaver 4.0 fast : rapid Web development. –
    (Essential series)
    1. Dreamweaver (Computer file)
    I. Title II. Dreamweaver 4.0 fast
    005.7'2
    ISBN 1852335734

Library of Congress Cataloging-in-Publication Data
A catalog record for this book is available from the Library of Congress

Essential Series ISSN 1439-975X
ISBN 1-85233-573-4 Springer-Verlag London Berlin Heidelberg
a member of BertelsmannSpringer Science+Business Media GmbH
http://www.springer.co.uk

Typesetting: Mac Style Ltd, Scarborough, N. Yorkshire
Printed and bound at The Cromwell Press, Trowbridge, Wiltshire
34/3830-543210 Printed on acid-free paper SPIN 10860525

Dedication

To my parents whose affection, support and prayers have made this possible.

Acknowledgements

I am indebted to Dr John Cowell, De Montfort University, for his excellent support and guidance throughout the development of this manuscript. I am also grateful to the team at Springer-Verlag for their assistance. In particular, I would like to thank Beverley Ford and Rebecca Mowat for their understanding, helpful suggestions, and for being just super people to work with. Final word goes to my family, who have taken the back seat to make time for me to write this book. To my wife, Shabana, and my two children, Luqman and Batool a big thank you.

Preface

The immense popularity of the Internet and, particularly, the World Wide Web (web, for short) has meant that more and more businesses are making an effort to use this medium to publish and promote their activities and products. The move from paper to an electronic form for business exposure is not always straightforward and, usually, some level of computer programming (which is often seen as restrictive) is required to develop professional web sites.

Macromedia® Dreamweaver® 4.0 provides a comprehensive visual environment that facilitates fast generation of web pages and sites, with minimal programming know-how. We can work with a number of tools, menu options, and panels to quickly design, formulate and realize a site. The development environment has a range of features to test, check and debug a web page or a web site. We can, in addition, choose to work with HTML codes or scripts (both JavaScript and VBScript are supported). These can be used, for example, to better control components forming a web page. Moreover, we can choose just to work with the visual form, or code only, or use both visual and code to develop a desired web page or web site.

The goal of this manuscript is to provide a fast insight to the numerous features and tools that Dreamweaver 4.0 offers. We will look at tables, cells, layers and frames as a means of realizing a desired page layout. The two key components for page content, namely text and pictures, have dedicated chapters. We will learn how to add, edit and publish such content. Links and hyperlinks are also covered and the way these can be realized through using the visual form is explain by virtue of examples. In addition, we will look at the generation of forms and how style sheets can be created and employed to assist in adding conformity to a site. The manuscript finally shows how to check, test and correct the content of a page or site, together with discussion on debugging code (especially, scripts). We will also learn how the environment assists us to evaluate, manage and publish our sites. The discussion throughout the manuscript is levied at providing a practical, visual and quick introduction to Dreamweaver 4.0.

It goes without saying that writing a book of such a dimension can always be improved. I would therefore welcome any comments and suggestions, together with notification of any omissions. My email address is `fiaz@ieee.org` and I look forward to hearing from. Wishing you every success with Dreamweaver 4.0.

Fiaz Hussain,
April 2002.

Contents

Contents

Chapter

1

Dreamweaver Environment

Introduction

Macromedia Dreamweaver 4.0 provides an exciting environment for creating and managing web pages and web sites. It has a range of tools and options that allow for fast and attractive generation. The design of web pages can be performed either through a visual editing environment where objects can be placed on a page as desired, or via HTML codes, or by a combination of both.

This chapter takes an introductory look at some of the components making-up the Dreamweaver 4.0 environment. In particular, we will look at:

● The toolbar
● The Objects panel
● The Property Inspector panel
● The launcher bar

The environment

On installing and running Dreamweaver 4.0, we are presented with a screen that typically looks similar to that shown in Figure 1.1. Macromedia provide two quick ways to get started, both of which are available through the Help submenu on the main menu: choosing Help | Guided Tour will activate six sessions which give an exposure to the environment; selecting Help | Lessons, on the other hand, returns seven lessons that interactively show how a basic web site could be developed.

As Figure 1.1 depicts, the Dreamweaver 4.0 interface consists of several components, some of which are identified in the figure. The document window is where the content of an active site (the one which is opened) is displayed. This, as we will see later in this chapter, can be used to show either a visual form or the actual code. The development of a site is assisted by the application of features that are available within a number of panels, including the Objects panel. This consists of a set of icons representing different types of objects that could be included in a site. It also has options for adjusting the manner in which we develop a site.

If we wanted to view and edit attributes belonging to an object, then we would use the Property Inspector panel. The range of options available on the panel is context driven in that different options appear for different selected objects. Also shown in Figure 1.1, are the toolbar and the launcher bar. Both provide quick access for features available within the main menu. For example, the toolbar can be used to select the display mode, whilst the launcher bar has a range of icons to open and close panels. We will look at each of these components in more detail, in this chapter, in order to familiarize ourselves with their respective features. Their actual usage will be demonstrated in the subsequent chapters.

One of the first steps towards using the environment is to ensure that the appearance, as well as the way objects will link with other aspects of a web site, are customized for the development at hand. To this regard, we use Edit | Preferences (or simply CTRL + U) to open the respective

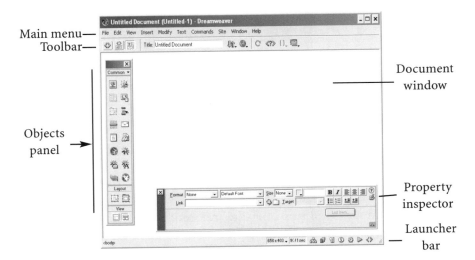

Figure 1.1 *The Dreamweaver 4.0 interface.*

dialogue box. As Figure 1.2 shows, the dialogue box has a series of options covering a number of categories. These include colour settings for the HTML code and the environment, specifying an external editor for creating and editing code, assigning default font and associated attributes, and highlighting invisible elements such as scripts. The dialogue box also offers the choice of establishing settings for layers such as size, the background and foreground colours for the cells and tables, as well as options for specifying the default browser, parameters for managing the web site, and deciding the contents for the status bar. We will be looking at most of these settings in the course of this book.

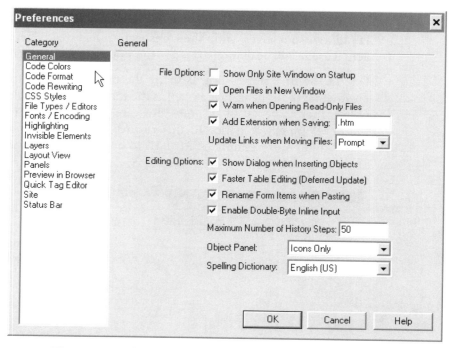

Figure 1.2 Preferences dialogue box, via Edit | Preferences.

In addition to using the preferences dialogue box, we can customize the settings for a (web) page through the page properties dialogue box. This is opened by choosing Modify | Page Properties and results in the dialogue box shown in Figure 1.3. As this figure shows, a number of adjustments can be made, including the title for the web page, insertion of a background picture which would be used as a wallpaper for a page, respective colours for text, links and background, as well as margin settings, and the way images are displayed. We will be looking at these options in detail in Chapter 2.

The toolbar

A set of buttons on the toolbar allow for fast access for some of the most common commands required in the development of a web document. To open the toolbar, we choose View | Toolbar, from the main menu. Figure 1.4 depicts the scenario; whilst Figure 1.5 shows the toolbar.

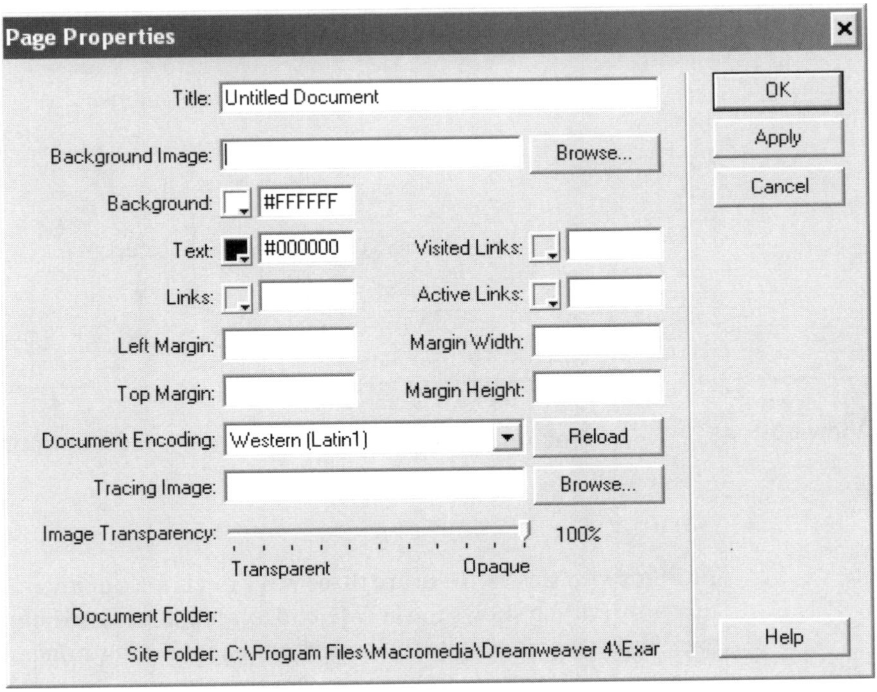

Figure 1.3 Page Properties dialogue box.

Figure 1.4 *Displaying the toolbar via the main menu.*

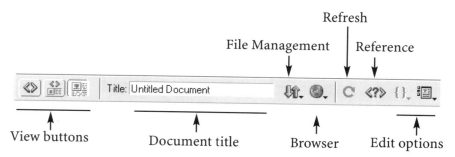

Figure 1.5 *The toolbar.*

As Figure 1.5 shows, there are three ways to view a document: text only (which shows the HTML codes, for example), design view only (which shows the components, including images, making-up a web page), and a combination of the two. Clearly, this allows the option of designing and editing a web document either by hand-coding or using visual components, or as we will see through a mixture of both. The respective buttons on the toolbar for selecting each display are shown below:

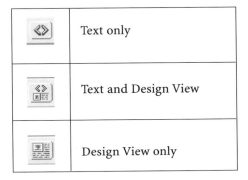	Text only
	Text and Design View
	Design View only

All three display options can also be activated through the View menu on the main menu. For example, choose View | Design to work solely in design view. We can also toggle between text only and design view only modes by either View | Switch Views, or through CTRL + Tab.

Whilst in design view only or text + design view modes, we can also work with rulers and grids. These are provided to aid the design process. To include horizontal and vertical rulers, we choose View | Rulers and then Show. As Figure 1.6 illustrates, the dimensions for the rulers can be set as pixels, inches, or centimetres.

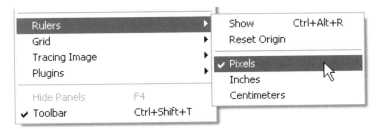

Figure 1.6 *Selecting a unit dimension for the rulers.*

The option Reset Origin, in Figure 1.6, refers to the fact that the origin (0,0) can be adjusted from its default location (which is top-right hand corner of a document window). To do this, we select the ruler-origin icon and drag it to a desired position. Figure 1.7 provides an animated illustration. The option Reset Origin, therefore, returns the origin to its default location.

Origin
icon —

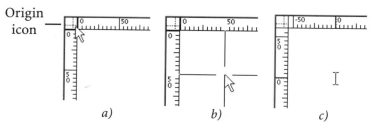

a)   b)   c)

Figure 1.7 *Adjusting the ruler origin (0,0): (a) original, (b) icon being dragged, and (c) being placed at a new location.*

The grids provide a useful way of laying out the objects on a page. Either through manual position or by means of the snap to option, objects can be aligned to meet specific page design requirements. We can turn on (and off) the grids by selecting View | Grid and then Show Grid. In a similar manner, the snapping option is activated by choosing View | Grid and then Snap to Grid. These options are also available within the Grid Settings dialogue box. This can be opened by selecting View | Grid and then Edit. The resulting dialogue box is shown in Figure 1.8. As this figure shows, we can

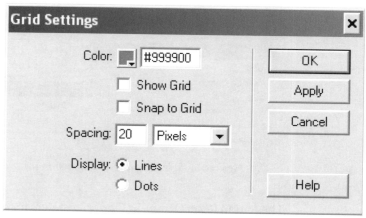

Figure 1.8 *Grid Settings dialogue box.*

choose the colour of the grids, the spacing in terms of pixels or inches or centimetres, and whether to use lines or dots to display the grid. The Apply button provides a useful way of deciding upon the most appropriate settings prior to accepting them (by clicking OK).

The other button on the toolbar to mention at this stage is the one labelled as Browser (in Figure 1.5). As the name suggests, this is used to launch the default browser for either viewing or debugging the current document. Figure 1.9 shows the menu associated with the Browser button. The Edit Browser List opens up the preference dialogue box, with the category Preview in Browser selected and allowing default browser settings to be adjusted.

Figure 1.9 *Browser options on the toolbar.*

The Objects panel

Dreamweaver 4.0, like other products by Macromedia, allows the creation and editing of objects, be it text or image, through a set of panels. We can open and close panels via the Window submenu, on the main menu. As Figure 1.10 shows, there are a number of panels covering a range of attributes. We will look at the Objects panel in this section and the Properties panel in the next. As we will see, these two provide us with a framework to develop a basic web page. The other panels we will look at in subsequent chapters.

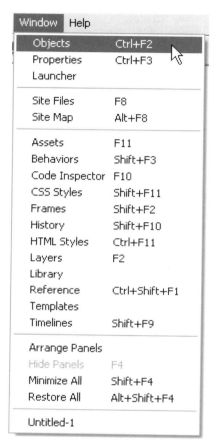

Figure 1.10 *Available panels within the Windows menu.*

As the name suggests, the Objects panel allows insertion of a range of objects into a document. These include static and dynamic (animation) pictures, files from Flash or Fireworks or other listed application software programs, hyperlinks and email links, text and special characters, layers, forms, tables and cells, etc.

As implied in Figure 1.10, we open the Objects panel by choosing Window | Objects. Depending upon the default settings, the resulting panel would display options either in terms of button icons only, or text only, or a combination of the two. The display variations are shown in Figure 1.11.

These variations can be selected through the preferences dialogue box (Edit | Preferences). We then choose the General category. Within this, there is an option that refers to the Objects panel (display) settings. By selecting one of the three modes, we are then able to change the panel display settings as desired.

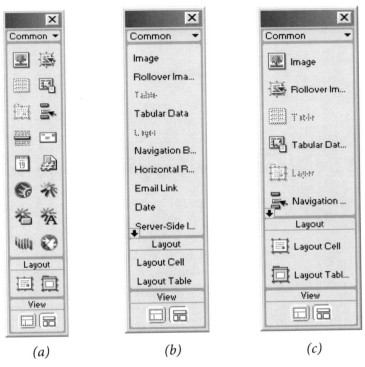

(a) (b) (c)

Figure 1.11 Objects panel in: (a) icon only, (b) text only, and (c) icon + text display modes.

The Objects panel has by default seven categories. Each category has a set of options associated with it to allow quick insertions to be made for a document. The default categories are Characters, Common, Forms, Frames, Head, Invisibles and Special. We choose a category by using the pop-up menu at the top of the Objects panel. This is illustrated in Figure 1.12.

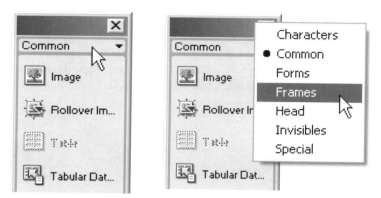

Figure 1.12 Choosing a category for the Objects panel.

The Property Inspector panel

The Objects panel provides a convenient way of adding objects into a document. The Property inspector, on the other hand, allows for attributes associated with a object to be examined and to be edited. The range of options available will vary depending upon the type of object that is selected. We invoke the Property Inspector panel via `Window | Properties`. An example of the resulting panel is shown in Figure 1.13.

When an object is selected and the Property Inspector panel invoked, the range of options shown on the panel are those that are used frequently for the selected object. Depending upon the selected object, additional options may be available. To view these, we use the compress/expand button (see Figure 1.13). This acts as a toggle for viewing either additional features or the most frequently used. For assistance in understanding the options available within the Property Inspector panel for a selected object, we can click on the button marked '?' (which is located in the top-right corner of the panel). This opens the relevant pages through the Help window.

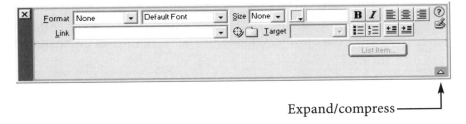

Expand/compress

Figure 1.13 The Inspector property panel.

The launcher bar

In common with other Macromedia products, the Dreamweaver 4.0 environment has a launcher bar. This provides fast access to frequently used panels, inspectors and windows. We can display the launcher bar either within the status bar, or as a separate window. To do the former, we make use of the preferences dialogue box. As mentioned earlier, to open the preferences dialogue box, we choose `Edit | Preferences`. Within the dialogue box, we select the Status Bar as the category. From the available options, check the one labelled as Launcher. Figure 1.14 depicts the scenario.

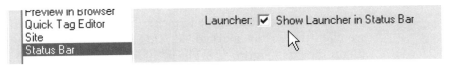

Figure 1.14 Using the Preferences dialogue box to open the launcher bar within the status bar.

The resulting launcher bar is shown in Figure 1.15, where the button icons refer to the respective panels, inspectors, and windows.

To open the launcher bar as a separate window, we choose `Window | Launcher`. This invokes a window containing the button icons, as illustrated by Figure 1.16. The figure also indicates that the orientation of this window, whether horizontal or vertical, can be adjusted. We use the button (shown in Figure 1.16 and which is located at the bottom-right of the window) to toggle between the two orientations.

Launcher Bar

Figure 1.15 Launcher bar embedded in the status bar.

Switch orientation

Figure 1.16 Launcher bar (horizontal) window.

By default, the launcher bar contains a set of button icons representing the panels, inspectors, and windows. We can add, remove and also adjust the position of the icons. To do this, we open the preferences dialogue box (Edit | Preferences) and then Panels as the category. The portion that is of interest to us is shown in Figure 1.17. The text box, in the middle of Figure 1.17, shows the current list of button icons that will appear in the launcher bar. To add to this list, we click the button marked '+'. This results in the pop-up menu shown in Figure 1.18. The items already included in the launcher bar are greyed-out, allowing the others to be inserted into the list. The button with the minus label '-' is there to remove any selected items from the list.

In addition, we can adjust the ordering of items in the list, which in turn changes the position of the icons within the launcher bar. By moving an item towards the top, it moves the icon (for a horizontal window) towards the left. So that the top listed item has its icon on the far left on the launcher bar. Moving the same item downward in the list will shift the icon towards the right. We can move a item up or down by selecting it from the list and using the respective arrows (see Figure 1.17 for the positioning of the arrows). Any changes made to the panel list are shown once we close the preferences dialogue box (by clicking OK).

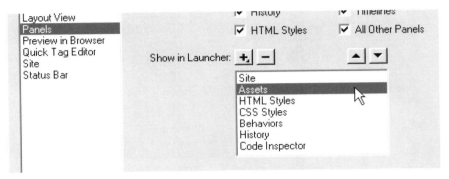

Figure 1.17 Options for adding, removing and positioning the panels, available within the Preference dialogue box.

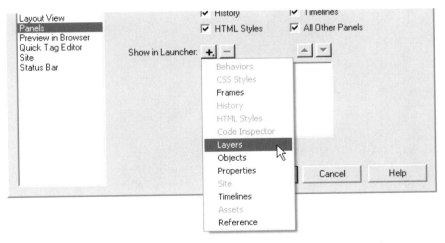

Figure 1.18 Pop-up menu for adding button icons to launcher bar.

Chapter
2

Dreamweaver Basics

Introduction

The first step to producing a web site is to plan its structure and to organize its contents. In doing so, we are defining the primary audience and, most importantly, the way the components of the web site would be used. We also need to identify a location where the resulting files would reside and the relationship, if any, the respective files will have with each other. Though this appears to be a trivial point, it is in fact a critical element for designing, sharing and managing web pages within a development such as that offered by Dreamweaver 4.0.

This chapter shows how we can quickly establish a framework for our web site, defining folders and files and their respective relationships, if any. Through this we learn the various features that Dreamweaver 4.0 offers to develop, monitor, analyze and manage a web site project.

Creating a site structure

Dreamweaver 4.0 works with defining a site for a production. Whether the resulting web site is for providing personal information or for a business requirement, the web pages need to be stored and their intra-relationships established. By site, Dreamweaver 4.0 refers to the actual web pages or their storage location, or both.

The creation of a site is similar to other environments where a project folder (or directory) is formed and all the relevant files stored therein. A hierarchical structure is then realized where a main folder links to sub-folders to produce a workable project.

In the world of Dreamweaver 4.0, the main folder is referred to as the root directory, where other sub-folders and files span. We can plan a site structure and create the relevant folders and files and then designate a site, or we can do things the other way round by defining a site and then producing the respective documents. Each web site will have a corresponding root directory.

The structure of the site is commonly predetermined by the designer, who produces the files and then stores them on a local storage device (for example, hard disk), within a folder and linked sub-folders. The result is what is referred to as the local site. A copy of this is then uploaded onto a server for publication.

As we will see, Dreamweaver 4.0 provides a flexible environment for specifying a local site, either at the initiation phase of the development, or at any intermediate stage, or even after completion of a site. The key point being that the environment supports the creation of new folders and files.

Creating a local site

So, how do we set-up a new local site for a web production? We start by making use of the Site Definition dialogue box. This can be opened in a variety ways, the most convenient and straightforward being Site | New Site. Figure 2.1 shows the resulting dialogue box.

The dialogue box contains a number of options for customizing the settings to meet our requirements. To set-up a local site, do the following:

- Within the Category list, choose Local Info.
- Enter the name of the site in the text field for Site Name. The name is used for reference within Dreamweaver 4.0 and is not used as a title, for example, by a browser. Let us call our site Dreamweaver Examples. Figure 2.2 depicts the scenario.
- Specify the path to the (main) local folder in the text field for Local Root Folder. This is the root directory and as such has within it all relevant files for the site. The icon next to the text field can be used to browse to a particular folder, or even create a new folder within a desired

location on the local storage. Figure 2.3 shows an animated illustration of creating a root folder.

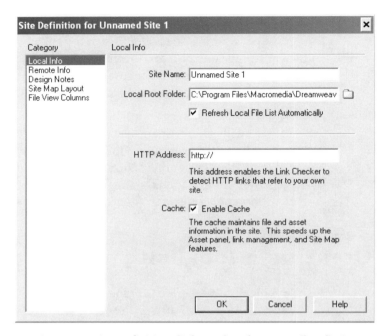

Figure 2.1 *Site Definition dialogue box for a new (local) site.*

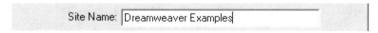

Figure 2.2 *Specifying a site name.*

● Check the Refresh Local File List Automatically option to provide for an up-to-date view of the site. As the name suggests, when there is a change in the number of files within a site, this option will automatically update the list – allowing for site maps, for example, to reflect the current state of play.

● If the URL for the finished web site is known, then enter this in the text field for HTTP Address. This is used by Dreamweaver 4.0 to check and verify links, particularly URLs that are referred to as being absolute. If the URL is not known then at this stage we can leave the text field blank.

- To improve system performance, the Cache box can be checked. This creates a record of the files comprising a site and helps, for example, to quickly update links to any filename changes or deletes. Moreover, the Assets panel can only be used if this option is selected. The Assets panel is presented later in this chapter.
- Having entered and chosen the various options, we can choose OK to accept these and close the dialogue box.

(a) Choose folder button to open dialogue box.

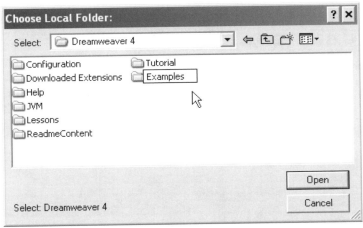

(b) Enter a name for the root folder (Examples) and choose Open and then Select.

(c) The path to the root folder is then displayed within the Local Root Folder text field.

Figure 2.3 *Creating a root folder for a site, using the Definition Site dialogue box.*

Having chosen to create a cache version of our site, Dreamweaver then prompts to say that it is about to do this. Figure 2.4 shows the prompt message. Click OK to accept.

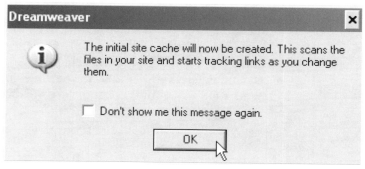

Figure 2.4 *Create site cache dialogue box.*

Understanding the site map

With a local site established, we are just about ready to develop its contents. Before we do this, it is worth looking at some components of the Dreamweaver 4.0 environment that allow for analyzing and managing site files and folders.

One of the primary components for this is the site window. This can be opened via any of the following ways:

- By creating a local root folder (as shown above). After generating the cache version, the Dreamweaver 4.0 environment automatically opens the site window.
- By clicking Site | Site Files or Site | Site Map.
- By selecting Site | Open Site, and then the desired site (name). Figure 2.5 shows the example where we want to open the site window for our newly created (Dreamweaver Examples) local site.
- We can also choose to open the site window through the Define Sites window. We activate the Define Sites window by choosing Site | Define Sites. The resulting window is shown in Figure 2.6, where a list of sites is presented. Various options are available to us: we can

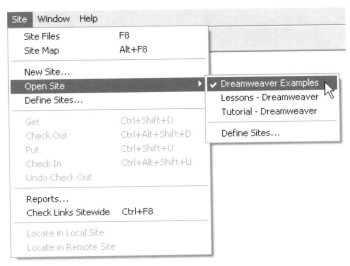

Figure 2.5 *Opening a site window for a specified site.*

choose to create a new site by clicking the New button, or to edit a selected site through the Edit button. Both of these take us to the Site Definition dialogue box (discussed in the previous section). We can make a copy of a site by using the Duplicate option, or to delete a site by selecting the Remove button. To view the site window, we highlight the desired site and then click Done.

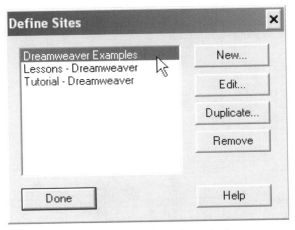

Figure 2.6 *The Define Sites window.*

The site window that is opened using any of the above listed approaches is shown in Figure 2.7. The window is titled using the name of the site entered in the Site Definition dialogue box. Since we have created a new local site which to date contains no files or folders, the window simply displays the root folder (and its path). We can see from Figure 2.7 that by default the site window is split into two sections: on the right hand pane are the details of the local files and folders used for the site, whilst on the left hand pane are the contents of the remote site. At this stage, we are working with generating a local site, so we will defer the discussion on the remote site until this has been generated (see Chapter 11). Though we are looking at the Dreamweaver Examples site, we can view other sites by using the pull-down menu shown in Figure 2.8.

As far as the working of the site window is concerned, this is very similar to using, for example, Windows Explorer. We can therefore execute, cut, paste, delete, move, rename, etc, the items listed under the Local Folder. The space occupied by each of the two panes (and by the respective columns) can be adjusted using the column dividers. Figure 2.9 gives an

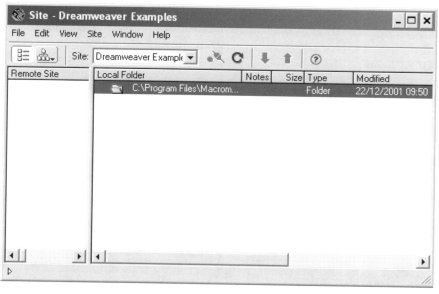

Figure 2.7 The site window.

animated illustration for the two panes, where the size has been adjusted using the familiar click and drag approach. As we will see in the subsequent chapters, the site window provides a wealth of features to analyze and manage sites.

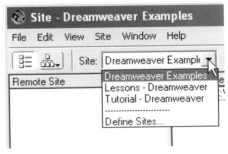

Figure 2.8 Pull-down menu allows for specifying a current site.

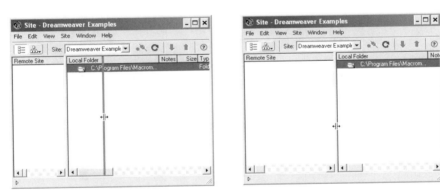

Figure 2.9 Adjusting the view size of the two panes.

Understanding site assets

As we begin to develop our web site, a number of files will be used to generate the various components of the site. These may come from a variety of sources and could take the form of text, picture, sound, or video files. Typically, these are generated using suitable application packages and are made available for inclusion in the site. Dreamweaver 4.0 refers to such elements as assets. So, we can think of creating our web site using a series of assets.

To assist the designer, assets are organized and presented in a corresponding window, referred to as the Assets panel. The panel can be opened using `Window | Assets`, or by pressing the function key F11, or by means of the launcher bar. Figure 2.10 depicts the scenario for the last option where a corresponding button is used to open the Assets panel. All three options act as toggles and therefore can also be used to close the panel.

The Assets panel for the Dreamweaver Examples site is shown in Figure 2.11. As this manifests, we choose a category to view and, also, whether to view all assets of the site or to constrain the viewing to only the favourites. Figure 2.12 depicts the respective labels for each of the categories. As a site is developed, the list of assets is generated automatically to be displayed in the panel. This is viewed through the view Site option. Favourite assets are created manually as a project develops. Apart from organizing the various assets, the panel also provides a way of reusing items as and when required.

Figure 2.10 *Using the launcher bar to open the Assets panel.*

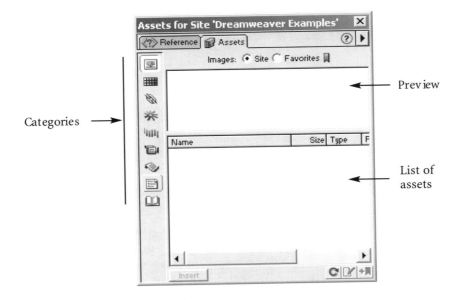

Categories

Preview

List of assets

Figure 2.11 The Assets panel.

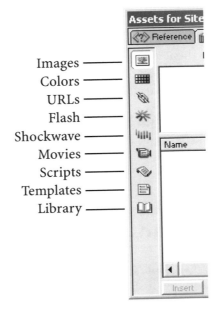

Images
Colors
URLs
Flash
Shockwave
Movies
Scripts
Templates
Library

Figure 2.12 List of categories for the Assets panel.

Understanding templates

Templates are a convenient way of developing pages with consistent look and feel, where the backbone to the site is the template. In other words, a template can be used as a basis for designing and developing a multitude of pages, with the template acting as a guideline for content layout. The employment of templates is especially useful when the development of a site involves a number of personnel. Templates can be designed by one person and can be made available to others to use for their part of the development.

The Dreamweaver 4.0 environment supports the concept and usage of templates through the Assets panel. Typically, when a site is defined, the environment creates a template folder in the root directory. The original files for a template are stored here, with an extension of 'dwt'. A copy of this is then used whenever a page employs the template.

Templates consist of two primary sections; namely editable or locked. A page making use of a template must consist of either an editable part, or locked part, or both. Normally, when a template is created, all its areas are defined as locked. We then define editable regions that can change from page to page. These areas (or sub areas) can be relocked on a page. We can also, after developing a page via a template, remove the link between the page and the template and therefore be able to edit those sections that were locked. A page can be linked again to the same or a different template, but this may affect the way the page contents are displayed depending on the locked areas.

Creating and using templates

We can gain a template by either using an existing page design or through creating a new template from scratch. In the case of the former, we design a page as normal and then convert the final version to a template. To do this, choose

File | Save as Template. This opens the dialogue box shown in Figure 2.13. Here, we can choose the site from the pull down menu and name the template as required. Clicking on the Save button will store the template with a 'dwt' extension, in the site root directory. The page title changes to reflect that it is now a template. As Figure 2.14 shows, the

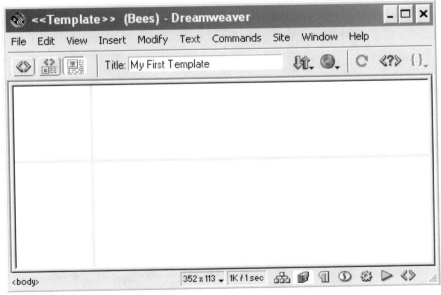

Figure 2.13 *Dialogue box for converting page into a template.*

Figure 2.14 *Conversion of a page to a template.*

name of the template is included in brackets on the title
header, as well as <<Template>> label.

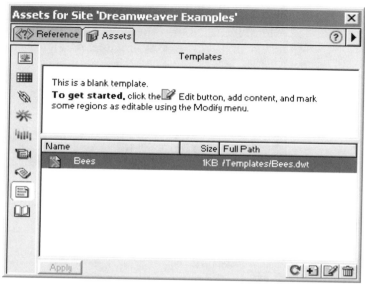

Figure 2.15 *Assets panel showing available templates.*

Once the conversion has taken place, the Assets panel is
automatically updated to register the new template. To view
this, click on the Templates category on the panel (see Figure
2.12). The Assets panel, as Figure 2.15 depicts, then displays
the newly created template as an item that can be used similar
to other assets. We need then to define the editable regions for
the template. Discussion on this is given later in this section.

To create a template from scratch, choose Window |
Templates. This will open the Assets panel with the
Templates category selected. Click on the New Template
button (located bottom right, with a plus sign on it) to
create a new blank template. This, as Figure 2.16 shows, is
added to the Assets panel with an option of renaming the
template.

As mentioned earlier, we must create editable regions to
make the template useful since a new template has all its
areas locked. The steps necessary for this are as follows:

- Choose a template from the Assets panel and then select the Edit button. The button is located on the right of the New Template button.
- Next select `Modify | Templates` and then New Editable Regions.
- Type in a suitable name for the template in the dialogue box that opens. The environment displays the name of the template on the page, surrounded by braces and using the colour settings specified in the preferences dialogue box (under Highlighting category). Figure 2.17 shows an example. This acts as a placeholder for page content (text, picture, etc).

We lock a region by removing its editable feature by choosing `Modify | Templates` and then Remove Editable Region.

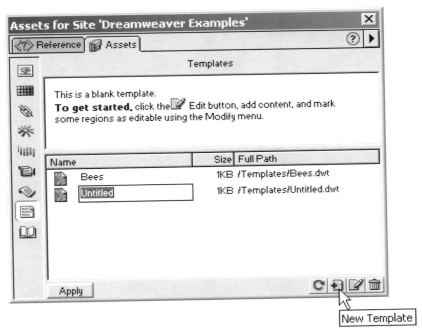

Figure 2.16 Creation of an empty template.

Figure 2.17 Placeholder for an editable region.

To use a template for a new page, select File | New from Template and then a desired template from the resulting dialogue box. Alternatively, click on the Apply button on the Assets panel to use the selected template on a new or existing document.

Chapter

3

Working with Cells and Tables

Introduction

The two previous chapters have identified some key components that make up the Dreamweaver 4.0 development environment. These provide the basis for creating a site and in this chapter we begin the journey of planning and designing a web site. We focus on understanding the two visual forms that allow for this, namely Standard view and Layout view. The discussion centres on showing the way cells and tables (and their respective attributes) can assist in the design of a site. Where appropriate, examples are provided to show how quickly a page layout, and therefore a web page, could be generated.

Understanding web page design

Next in deciding on the structure of a site, what and where files and folders will reside, is the actual layout and positioning of elements on a (web) page. This clearly is important since it will determine not just the way the page will look, but also the way the users will interact with our site.

A page typically is laid out to be presentable within a target browser or browsers. Every element has a placeholder on page. The banner, the menu, the heading, the text, the pictures, etc, are all placed on a page at a desired location. This way, we can control not just the contents, but also the positioning of each of the components making up the contents. It is not surprising therefore that the Dreamweaver 4.0 environment provides a number of ways to control and manage the layout of a page.

Of particular note is the use of tables and cells. These traditionally have been used to present and organize table data, so their transformation to being a page layout tool is not always straightforward. The Dreamweaver 4.0 visual environment, as we will see in this chapter, provides an efficient way of planning and arranging elements on a page using tables and their cells.

As Figure 3.1 shows, when it comes to using tables for page layout, we should consider the rows and columns as providing respectively vertical and horizontal spacing, and their corresponding intersections (that is, the cells) as placeholders for our elements (such as text or pictures). With tables we are therefore in a position to place elements within cells and to space the elements on a page. We can, of course, use the corresponding attributes of cells to pad and to space contents between and within cells as well.

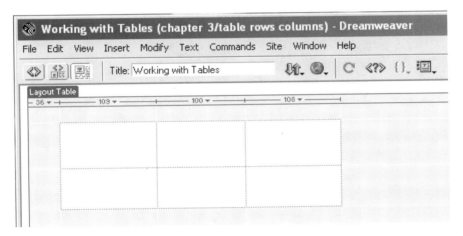

Figure 3.1 *Table returns horizontal and vertical space on a page.*

Choosing a layout view

As mentioned earlier, Dreamweaver 4.0 provides two ways of establishing and working with a page design. These are called Standard view and Layout view. Both work with tables and cells, though the Layout option provides the best starting point. As Figure 3.2 depicts, we can choose either design modes through the Objects panel. Alternatively, as Figure 3.3 shows, we can choose View | Table View and then the desired design view.

We can start the design of a web page through the Layout view and then use the Standard view to complete it. Each design view has specific attributes associated with it. As an early taster for the distinct features of each, let us look at Figures 3.4 and 3.5. In Figure 3.4, we are working in the Layout view and have drawn three cells (we will learn later in this chapter how to do this). The corresponding attributes are shown in the Property Inspector panel. Changing the design view to Standard results in Figure 3.5. The size and positions of the three cells have been used to create a table, consisting of 4 rows and 4 columns. We can, in fact, use any of the cells shown in Figure 3.5 and not just the three created in the Layout view. For example, we can insert text or change colour

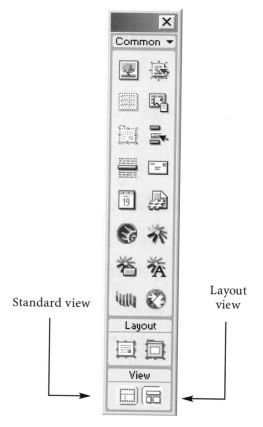

Figure 3.2 Design view options via the Objects panel.

for each cell. Moreover, in Standard view, we can change row height or column width, whilst in Layout view we change individual cell height or width. In doing the latter, we create additional rows or columns.

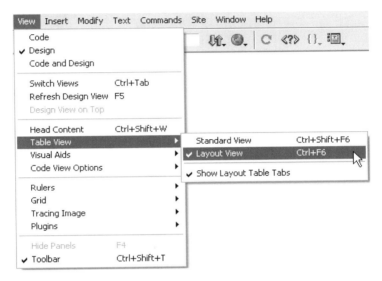

Figure 3.3 Design view selection through the main menu.

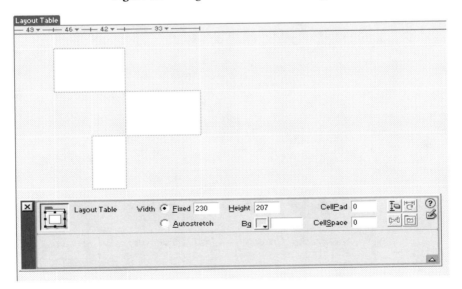

Figure 3.4 Creation of three cells in Layout view.

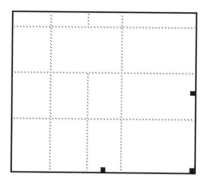

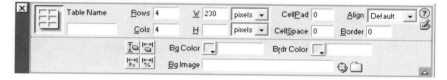

Figure 3.5 _Standard view of the three cells in Figure 3.4._

When in Layout view, we can choose to work with cells or tables to draw outlines of a web page. We can define a table and then subdivide it into cells, or draw using cells and convert the cells into a table. As Figure 3.6 depicts, two icons on the Objects panel are used to decide whether cells or tables are used for page layout.

Draw layout cell → 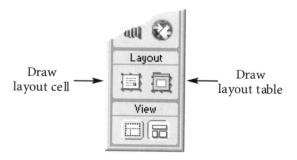 ← Draw layout table

Figure 3.6 _Draw cell and table icons on the Objects panel._

Designing a page layout

To understand the various features offered by Dreamweaver 4.0 for producing page layout, we will work through some examples. Let us assume that we want to create a page that has placeholders for a logo, a banner, a menu for three options, a text block and an image. We want to create a page layout similar to that shown in Figure 3.7.

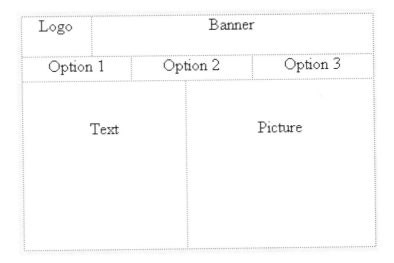

Figure 3.7 Desired layout for a web page.

As a first step, select Layout view and then Draw Layout Cell from the Objects panel. This allows for the creation of cells at a desired location, of a required size, on the document window. The mouse cursor changes shape to a crosshair so that we can position and drag to draw a cell of a specific height and width. Figure 3.8 provides an animated illustration of this for creating the placeholder for the logo, starting with selecting the cell icon, clicking and dragging for a cell size and then releasing for a desired cell size. After a cell has been drawn, the cursor changes to that of a (selection) pointer. The document window now becomes a (layout) table with the drawn cell and a shaded area covering the remaining parts of the window. Gridlines are automatically generated reflecting the horizontal and vertical coordinates of the cell. Figure 3.9 depicts the scenario. The gridlines provide a way of aligning other components on the page and become row and column dividers when the design view is changed to Standard. In fact, the gridlines subdivide the page into further cells that can be viewed as being inactive (that is, not being used) at this stage.

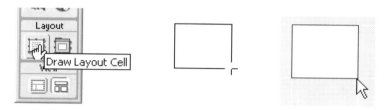

Figure 3.8 Creating a cell within the document window.

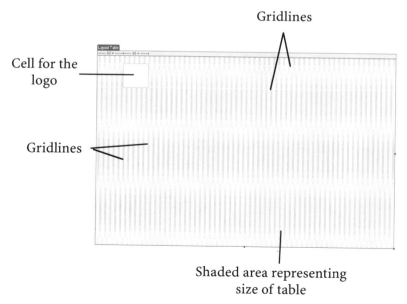

Figure 3.9 Document window, after a cell has been drawn.

We can position and size the (logo) cell more accurately by referring to actual dimensions. This can be achieved through a variety of ways, including using grids and rulers as discussed in Chapter 1. The layout table includes numbers horizontally placed at the top. These refer to column widths in pixels. Figure 3.10 depicts the case for the logo cell.

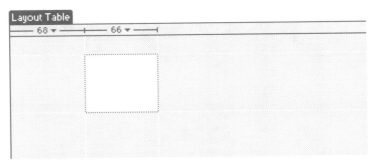

Figure 3.10 *Header of layout table shows column widths.*

The Property Inspector panel can also be used. For the scenario in Figure 3.10, the panel returns the output shown in Figure 3.11. We note that the panel, in fact, does not show any dimensions about the cell. What it gives are the overall height and width with reference to the top corner of the layout table, so that the width 134 is the sum of the column width 68 and the logo column width of 66. The height parameter in Figure 3.11 points to the lower edge of the logo cell from the top, in pixels.

Figure 3.11 *Property Inspector panel settings for the case shown in Figure 3.10.*

To get the dimensions for the logo cell, we must select the cell: the cell shown dotted will change to a solid outline to reflect that it can be selected. A single mouse click selects the cell, which is shown by a change of colour (from red to blue) and the emergence of eight small handles on the cell outline. Figure 3.12 gives an animated illustration of the selection process. If the mouse cursor was placed inside the cell and then clicked, the cell will not be selected. This will result in a text cursor appearing within the cell. More on this in the next chapter (Chapter 4). Selection of the cell can be made, however, if we had used the control (CTRL) key and then clicked whilst the mouse cursor was positioned inside a cell.

Figure 3.12 Animated illustration for selecting a cell.

Once the cell is selected, the Property Inspector panel displays parameters relevant to the cell. This is shown in Figure 3.13. The width and height parameters now return the pixel values for the cell.

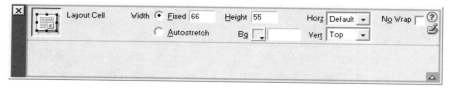

Figure 3.13 Property Inspector panel for the selected (logo) cell.

To resize the cell, we can choose to use the eight handles (four side and four corners) present when the cell is selected. In this case, the mouse cursor changes to a corresponding arrow shape to show that size changes can be made. Click and drag to re-adjust the size of the logo cell, if necessary. Alternatively, we can enter new values in the width and height parameters of the Property Inspector panel. The overall effect is the same in that the cell is re-sized. Figure 3.14 shows the case where the width and the height of the logo cell are changed to 70 and 60 pixels respectively.

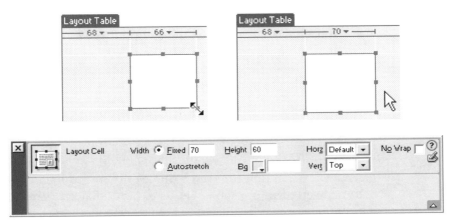

Figure 3.14 Cell resizing: manually and through the Property Inspector panel.

If a cell needs to be moved to a new location so that, for example, it lines up with another cell, then the first step is to select the cell. We can then choose to manually shift it by clicking and dragging or to use a combination of the Shift and cursor (arrow) keys. In the latter case, the Shift key will be held down and the arrow keys used to either move the cell up/down or left/right at interval of five pixels. Selecting the cell and using just the arrow keys results in single pixel increments.

Adding multiple cells

We can continue with developing our desired page layout (of Figure 3.7) by iterating the steps for creating, re-sizing and moving each cell as discussed in the previous section. This way, we create placeholders for each component (banner, menu options, text, etc). When wanting to add cells in a continuous manner, as for the menu, it is more convenient to use a shorthand. Instead of drawing a single cell and then going back to the Objects panel to repeat the task, we make use of the CTRL key. The way this works is as follows:

- From the Object panel, choose Layout view.
- Then select Draw layout cell icon from the Object panel.

- Press and hold down the CTRL key.
- Draw the first cell (as mentioned in the previous section) whilst holding down the CTRL key.
- Then draw the second and subsequent cells whilst continuing to hold down the CTRL key.

Working with individual cells is fine to a point. Often when designing, we need to work both at the micro (cell) and macro (group of cells) level. Dreamweaver 4.0 environment supports this concept by allowing individual cells to be grouped. When cells (or even a single cell) are grouped, they are converted into a table. Let us assume that we want to group the three cells created to hold the menu options. With reference to Figure 3.15, the steps to do this are as follows:

- From the Objects panel, choose Layout view.
- Then select Draw layout table icon (see Figure 3.6) from the Objects panel.
- Mark out an area that encompasses the three cells. We can do this, for example, starting at the top left corner of the first cell or bottom right corner of the third cell. By dragging diagonally across to the opposite corner, the three cells become selected.
- Once selected, the three cells become grouped as a table.

As Figure 3.15 suggests, the environment highlights possible cells that could be grouped as we start the selection process. We simply choose the cells that need to be part of the table. If the selection process had started outside the cells then the table would have included the cells and any shaded area that was covered. The point to note is that any adjustments in the attributes (for example, colour changes) will normally apply to the table as a whole, including any shaded areas. More on working with tables in the next section.

Understanding and using tables

Working with individual cells and then converting them to tables is one way of generating a page layout. Another way of

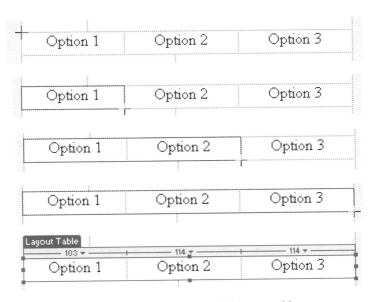

Figure 3.15 *Converting cells into a table.*

achieving similar goals is to start with a table and then to split it up into cells. In fact, looking at the previous section again, although we started with producing individual cells for our page, the environment automatically placed the cells in a table layout. This points to the fact that cells need to be placed inside a table.

Let us assume that we wish to re-create the basic page layout (shown in Figure 3.7), but this time by defining a table and then subdividing it into cells. The steps for creating a table are as follows:

● From the Objects panel, choose Layout view.
● Then select Draw layout table icon from the Objects panel. This tells the environment that we wish to work with tables rather than cells.
● Next position the mouse cursor to a desired location and click and drag to draw out a table of a desired size. Being the first table on the page, the environment will automatically position it with reference to the top left corner of the document window.

Figure 3.16 shows how the page will look once an initial table has been created. The dimensions at this stage are not important as these can be customized later. The table by default is drawn with a green outline, just like the cell has a solid red outline to show that it can be selected. We can choose to change the default settings such as the colours by selecting `Edit | Preferences`. This, as mentioned in Chapter 1, opens the preferences dialogue box. In order to make changes to the table outline colour, we choose the Layout View from the Category list. We need then to make use of the Table Outline parameter to either change the colour through a palette or by entering a hexadecimal combination in the provided text field. In the case of the latter, enter values respectively for red, green, and blue (two hexadecimal digits per colour) as commonly used to define colour combinations. Figure 3.17 shows the case where the colour palette has been opened to select a new colour for the table outline.

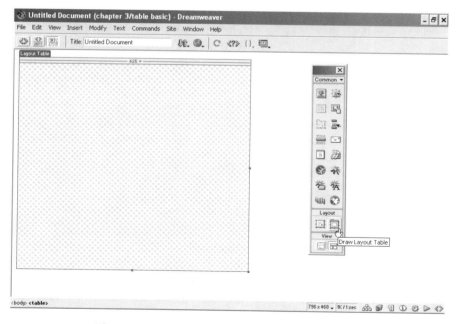

Figure 3.16 Creation of an initial table on a page.

We can add cells and additional tables on to the page, but these can only be inserted within the initial table. Similar to cells, where we can align but not directly superimpose, tables cannot overlap with each other either. To aid development, the environment automatically aligns cells and tables to each other when they are reasonably close together. The snap on feature works with cells only, tables only and with cells and tables. It also works by aligning to one of the four edges of a table. Using the Alt key can turn off the snap on feature. Hold down the Alt key while drawing a cell or a table to prevent it from snapping to either to a table edge or to another cell or table. The term nested tables are used when additional tables are included within a table. The size (number of rows and columns) of the nested tables is independent of the underlying table.

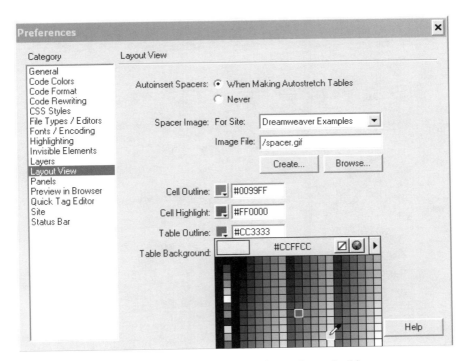

Figure 3.17 Changing the outline colour of tables through the preference dialogue box.

We can resize a table either through the Property Inspector panel or by using the handles attached to a table when it is selected. For the first (initial) table, we are presented with three handles since the top left corner is latched to the top of the page. In other words, we can change the width and depth of the table. As Figure 3.18 shows for a nested table, all eight handles are available for resize.

The tables are distinguished from cells on a page (apart from their respective drawing colours) by the fact that each table has a tab associated with it (see Figure 3.18). The tab is a useful attachment since it returns a quick means of selecting a table. It also provides an effective way of moving a table. Figure 3.19 depicts an animated illustration, where the click and drag approach is used to shift the table to a new position on the page. We can again make use of the arrow keys for single pixel movements of the table. Combining this with the

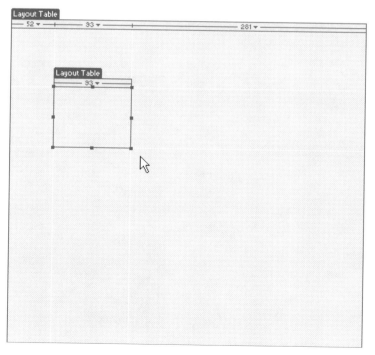

Figure 3.18 *Selection of a nested table, with 8 handles for resize.*

Shift key, results in movements of 10 pixels in the respective directions.

Let us return to producing the page layout of Figure 3.7. We can choose to use a table for each component to be placed on the page. That is, a table for the logo, a table for the banner, a

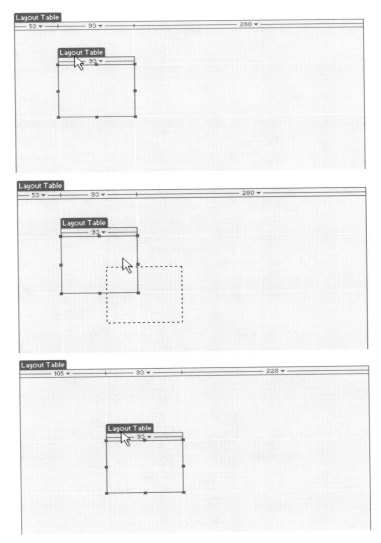

Figure 3.19 Moving table using the attached tab.

table each for the three menu options, a table to hold the text and a table for the picture. We could alternatively have three tables, the first consisting of the logo and banner, the second covering the menu options and the third for the text block and picture.

We will use the latter since it provides a balance between the number of tables and cells used to create the page. In an ideal situation, the first option would be chosen since tables provide better control over cells. In practice, however, a compromise between the number of tables and cells is often made.

We start the development with creating three tables for each of the sections mentioned above. The initial (layout) table will then contain three tables, similar to that shown in Figure 3.20. The sizes of the tables, again, are immaterial since these can and probably will need to be fine tuned to meet the desired outlook of the page. Note that all three tables are displayed with a dotted outline, are close enough to be automatically aligned and are unfilled (shaded).

To generate the placeholders for each of the page components, we make use of cells. The approach used to insert the cells in a table is the same as listed earlier (choose Layout view and then Draw layout cell from the Objects panel). Figure 3.21 shows the scenario where a cell (the first to be inserted) has been included for the text block. Note that this cell is shown as filled (with white colour). We can continue to create the remaining cells in the same manner, adjusting sizes and fine-tuning positions as desired. The final page layout would then look similar to that shown in Figure 3.22.

Although the width of cells and tables to date has been shown in pixels, there are occasions when designing web pages when it is preferable to work with percentages. Indeed, in many cases percentages are more appropriate as it is necessary to provide a relative (rather than fixed) width. The environment supports this viewpoint by having options to display column widths of a selected table in either pixels or percentages:

- To display pixels, choose Modify | Table and then Convert Widths to Pixels.
- To display percentages, choose Modify | Table and then Convert Widths to Percent.

Figure 3.23 depicts the scenario for both cases. It is worth noting that the cell width is a function of the total width of a table, including any space that may not be occupied by a cell.

Since both cells and tables are objects, with their respective set of attributes, it is important to know what takes precedence – the cell or the table properties? By default, the table parameters are used unless the cell is also specifying a similar attribute. For example, if the fill (background) colour for the table is set to blue and a cell had its colour set to red, then the cell will continue to have a red background whilst the remaining parts of the table would be blue.

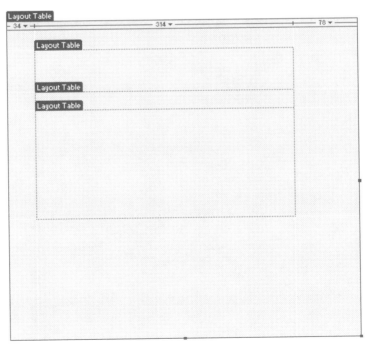

Figure 3.20 *Developing a page layout via nested tables.*

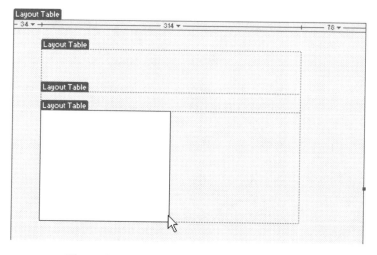

Figure 3.21 *Insertion of a cell within a table.*

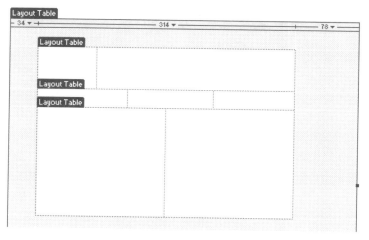

Figure 3.22 *Creation of page layout through tables and cells.*

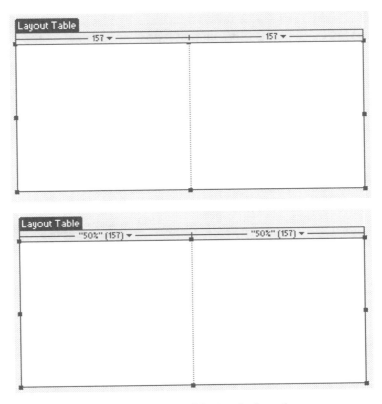

Figure 3.23 Table column widths: in pixels and percentages.

Using Standard View for tables

We have seen in the previous section how to produce a page layout through creating and editing tables and cells. We worked only in the Layout view and did not make use of the Standard view. In this section, we will look at some examples that will highlight the benefits of switching over to the Standard view. In order to make the discussion meaningful and practical, the basic page layout has had some content added to it. Figure 3.24 shows this in Layout view. We will learn in subsequent chapters how to enter content to a page. Looking at Figure 3.24, we note that the text block makes use of a table rather than a cell. This assists in controlling the size of text block so that it does not overrun the adjoining picture cell.

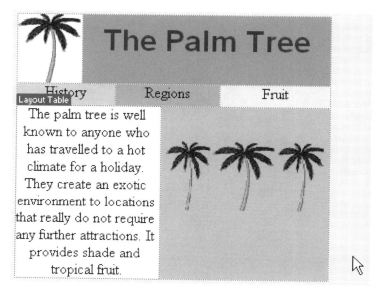

Figure 3.24 Basic page with content in Layout view.

We can switch to Standard view by simply selecting the Standard view icon on the Objects panel (see Figure 3.2). The document window containing the page will change to show the page in Standard view. This is depicted in Figure 3.25 (also Plate I). Looking at Figures 3.24 and 3.25, the display looks very similar with the content presentation unchanged. Moving to Standard view, however, means that we are now working with columns, rows and cells associated with the first (initial) layout table. Figure 3.25, in fact, implies this is where the page is shown to have six columns and four rows.

The cell width and height can be changed manually: we place the cursor on the respective cell boundary, then simply click and drag the boundary to a desired position. Figure 3.26 (also Plate I) provides an animated illustration of this, where the height of the row containing the menu is increased.

Figure 3.25 Basic page with content in Standard view (also Plate I).

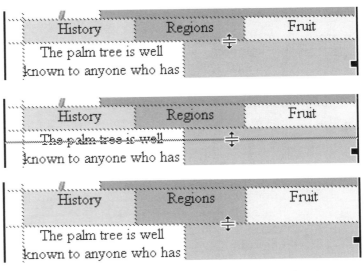

Figure 3.26 Increasing the row (menu options) height (also Plate I).

Cells can be merged and subdivided. We can combine cells either through the Property Inspector panel or via the main menu. To merge cells:

- Select cells to be combined.
- Either select Modify | Table and then Merge Cells, or
- Choose the merge button from the Property Inspector panel. This, as Figure 3.27 highlights, is located at the bottom left of the panel.

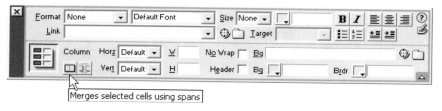

Figure 3.27 Using the Property Inspector panel to merge cells.

The process for splitting a cell is similar to that of merging cells. To split a cell:

- Select cell to be subdivided. A cell in this case is selected when the (insert) cursor is placed within it.
- Select Modify | Table and then Split Cells. This opens the dialogue box shown in Figure 3.28. We can choose to subdivide by inserting a specified number of rows or columns.
- Alternatively, the Property Inspector panel can be used to split cells. Figure 3.29 shows the split button on the panel to facilitate this. Selecting the button will activate the dialogue box shown in Figure 3.28.

We can also insert new rows or columns in a table, as well as remove existing ones. We can span across columns and rows (whose effect is similar to merging cells) and decrease span. The table menu shows these and other options that become available when a cell is selected. As mentioned earlier, we can open the table menu by choosing Modify | Table. In addition, the context menu can be used to achieve the same. Whilst the mouse cursor is positioned within a cell, click on the right mouse button and then choose Table. This opens up the table menu, an illustration of which is shown in Figure 3.30.

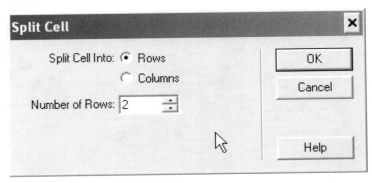

Figure 3.28 Split cell dialogue box.

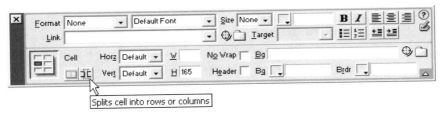

Figure 3.29 Using the Property Inspector panel to split a cell.

The Dreamweaver 4.0 environment also allows table contents to be vertically and horizontally aligned. We can align contents with respect to its border edges, or with reference to another cell content. For alignment, we use the Property Inspector panel. To vertically align, select a cell or cells, then choose an option from the corresponding pull-down menu. Figure 3.31 depicts the scenario, where we can align to top, middle, bottom, baseline, or to default. For horizontal alignment, we again select a cell or cells and then choose the desired option from the respective pull down menu. This is shown in Figure 3.32. In this case, we can choose to align to the left, center, right, or to default.

We can also specify the size of a cell or selected cells through the Property Inspector panel. As Figure 3.33 shows, we enter desired values in the respective text fields. Typically, we will

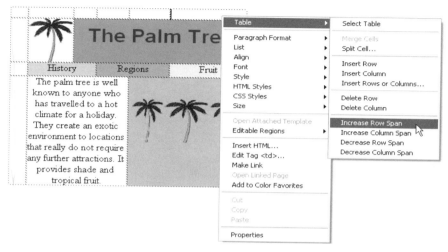

Figure 3.30 *Displaying table options via context menu.*

specify the number of pixels for the width and height, though we can also work with percentages by including a '%' character at the end of an entry.

We saw earlier, in the previous section, that the background colour of a cell, selected cells, or a table can be changed through using the corresponding option on the Property Inspector panel. The border colour for the table can also be changed: start with selecting the complete table and then use the Property Inspector panel to select a desired border colour. Unless a thickness for the border has been applied, we will not be able to view the border colour. A text field on the Property Inspector panel allows for sizing border widths in pixels. Figure 3.34 shows the respective border colour options.

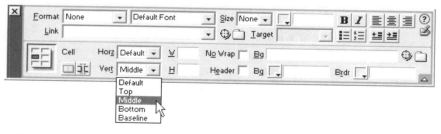

Figure 3.31 *Choosing a vertical alignment from the Property Inspector panel.*

Figure 3.32 Choosing a horizontal alignment using the Property Inspector panel.

Figure 3.33 Specifying the width and height of selected cell(s).

When working with cells, columns, rows, or a table as a whole, the Property Inspector panel includes a small, rather coarse, preview of how much and what has been selected. The word cell, row, or column is attached to the right of the preview. Figure 3.35 shows the three possibilities, where the top image shows cell, the middle, row, and the bottom image, column selection. The preview button can also be clicked to activate any changes made using the Property Inspector panel.

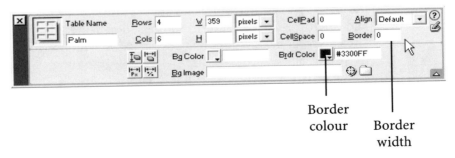

Border colour   Border width

Figure 3.34 Table border colour options, on the Property Inspector panel.

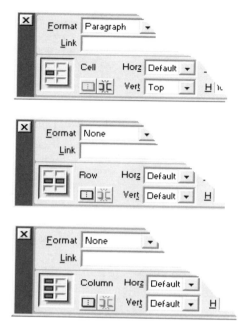

Figure 3.35 *Small preview of cell, row, or column selection.*

Using Autostretch for page layout

We have to date used the width attribute to set the dimensions of columns and therefore the total span of a page. This normally is expressed as pixels or percentages. There are clear advantages of specifying exact widths, though a more flexible approach is required to support different browsers and their respective screen settings. Realizing this, the Dreamweaver 4.0 environment supports two width settings: fixed and autostretch. We have already worked with fixed settings. In this section, we will focus on autostretch.

As the name suggests, the autostretch attribute allows for automatic adjustment of a cell width to cover the size of a screen. In other words, a cell marked as autostretch will expand (or contract) to fill the browser window – irrespective of the display settings. Autostretch is used on one selected column. Figure 3.36 shows the difference in displaying the same page using fixed and autostretch options with unchanged browser settings. In the example shown, the column containing the banner is set to autostretch.

To make a column autostretch, select Layout view from the Objects panel and then do the following:

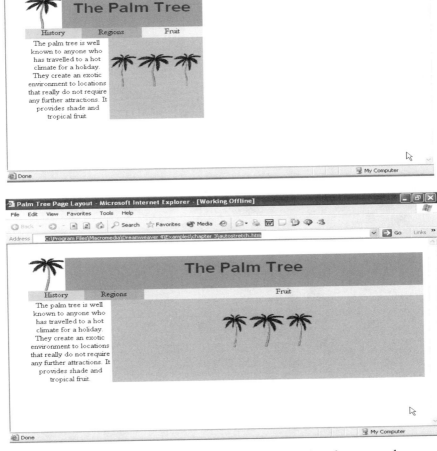

Figure 3.36 *Effect of using fixed width (top image) and autostretch.*

- Select a cell.
- From the Property Inspector panel, check the radio button labelled Autostretch. Figure 3.37 shows the position of the button.
- Alternatively, we can make use of the pull-down menu asociated with each column. This is located in the top bar (header) of the layout table. Figure 3.38 depicts the scenario.

When a column is designated to autostretch, the table header shows a wavy line in the corresponding column. Figure 3.39 provides an illustration of before (fixed) and after (autostretch) display of a column header. The right column is often set to autostretch since changes in its width least effects other columns.

Figure 3.37 Autostretch option on the Property Inspector panel.

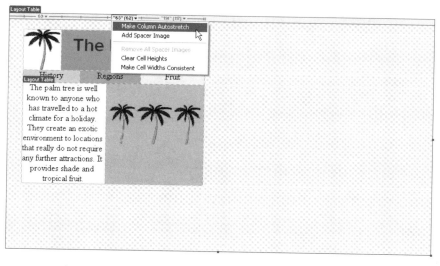

Figure 3.38 Autostretch option on the column header menu.

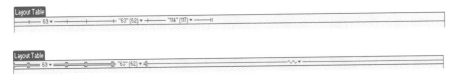

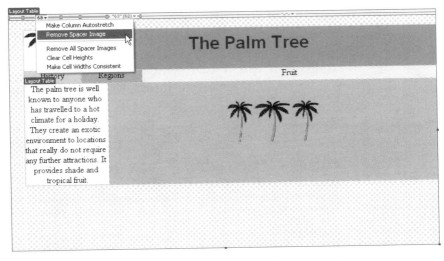

Figure 3.39 Right column: fixed width (top image) and autostretch.

Autostretch makes use of a spacer image to control spacing in tables. This is a transparent image, which is not visible in a browser, but is used to control the width of tables and cells. We can insert spacer images in columns or allow the environment to automatically create these when a column is made to autostretch. Columns, which make use of a spacer image, are displayed with a double bar within the column header. This is shown in Figure 3.40, where the option for removing the spacer image for the column (as well as for all others) is provided.

Figure 3.40 Double bar in the table header indicates use of spacer images.

When autostretch is selected from the Property Inspector panel, a corresponding dialogue box appears asking how to manage the spacer image file. As Figure 3.41 depicts, there are three options available:

- Create a spacer image file.
  Selecting this option will require a suitable location to save the spacer image file (spacer.gif).
- Use an existing spacer image file.
  If spacer.gif (or another spacer image file) already exists then we can choose this option.
- Don't use spacer images for autostretch tables.
  If the last is selected, a warning message appears. This says that columns are likely to collapse without spacer images. Width of columns would be related to their respective content.

It is recommended that the first option is chosen and, if a spacer image file already exists, then the second option. This way, the designed page layout will be maintained. Selecting the third option is clearly quite risky since columns with no content will collapse – affecting page layout. The preferences dialogue box (Edit | Preferences) has an option for specifying a spacer image for a desired site. Figure 3.42 shows the respective scenario, where the For Site parameter identifies a site (in our case Dreamweaver Examples) and a corresponding Image File. At this moment in time the respective text field is empty, though we could create or browse for a file. Alternatively, we can leave this blank and

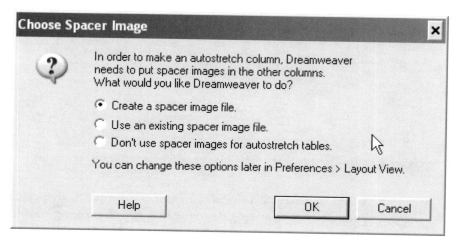

Figure 3.41 Spacer image dialogue box.

allow Dreamweaver 4.0 to automatically complete this when we want to make a column to autostretch. In fact, we would be offered the same dialogue box to create a new spacer image file when using autostretch or the create button located within the preferences dialogue box.

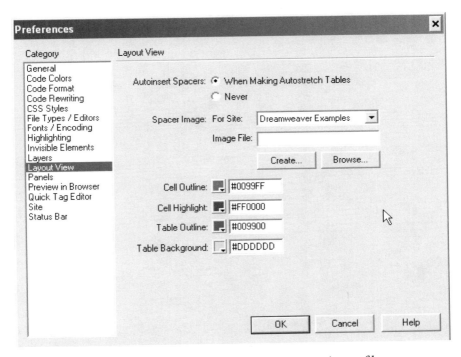

Figure 3.42 Option of including a site spacer image file.

Chapter

4

Working with Characters and Text

Introduction

The discussion thus far has focused on looking at key components of the Dreamweaver 4.0 environment to facilitate a fast development of a web page. We have seen how the Layout and Standard views on the Objects panel provide a convenient way of planning and designing a page. Through this, the important role of tables for page layout has been identified and their usage explained.

In this chapter, we begin to look at the content that makes up a web page. Though Dreamweaver 4.0 is a front end to putting together elements to develop a site, we will see in this chapter (and in subsequent chapters) the various tools provided to fine-tune content and to customize it for web usage. The primary purpose of this chapter, therefore, is to look at text and, in particular, the range of options available for including, editing and formatting characters and words.

Adding text to a page

We can add text to a page by one of two ways:

- either type the text directly into a document window or a table cell, or
- import it from another application package (such as Microsoft Word).

In this section, we will look at the first case, where a block of text is typed onto a page. This could be within a cell placeholder on the page, which itself is embedded in a table layout. Alternatively we can write directly on a document window. Figures 4.1 and 4.2 respectively show the two alternatives of including text in a page.

What happens if we wanted to include both types of insertion on a single page? Both can be accommodated. For a new page, if we typed in the document window first then the insertion of a cell will automatically commence after the inserted text.

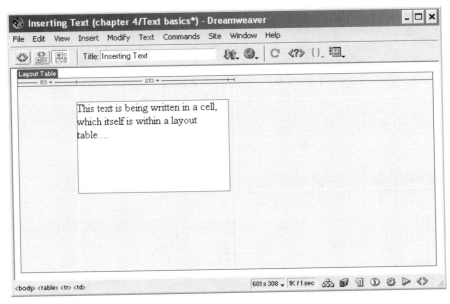

Figure 4.1 Insertion of text within a table cell.

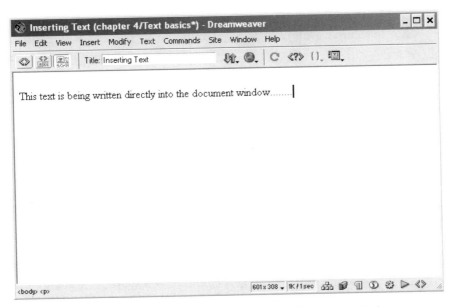

Figure 4.2 Insertion of text directly on to a document window.

Figure 4.3 depicts the scenario. If, however, we started with a layout table and a cell containing some text, then we will need to make use of the Standard view to add text to the document window. Within this view, we can position the cursor (and therefore any new text) either before or after the layout table. After typing in the new text, we can switch back to the Layout view. This should show the fact that the newly typed text is on the document window. Figure 4.4 illustrates the case of inserting new text after the layout table.

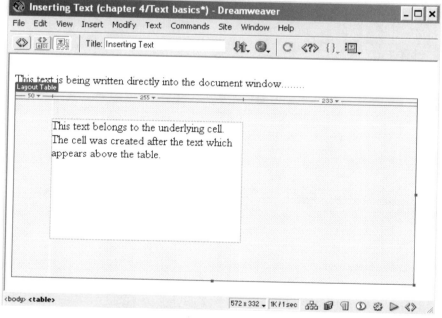

Figure 4.3 *Automatic position of table below the document window text.*

Importing text to a page

Alternatively, we can import a block of text created by another application (for example, MS Word) and use this as a basis of our content. The most convenient way of doing this is to use cut and paste. We simply run the other application and open the file containing the desired text. Next, select and either copy or cut the desired text. This places the selected text on the clipboard. Through placing the insertion cursor (point) at the desired location on the web page, we can use the paste command to insert the text. The paste command is located at Edit | Paste.

An example of inserting a text block is given in Figure 4.5. Here, the block has been written in MS Word, using a set of desired attributes. The cut and copy approach is then applied to move the text into the Dreamweaver 4.0 environment. Both the original text in MS Word and the pasted text are shown. We note that this approach does not maintain formatting. Apart from line breaks, commands for alignment, shading, bolding and underlining have all been forsaken. This is not a great loss since most, if not all, of the formatting commands are available within the Dreamweaver 4.0 environment. The next section provides an insight to the range of formatting options supported by the environment.

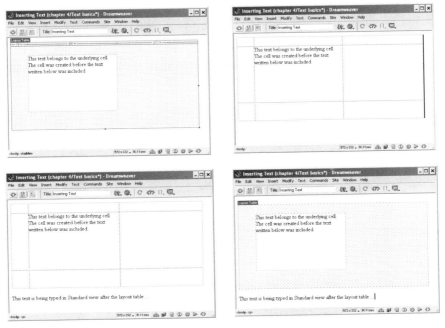

Figure 4.4 *Insertion of text below a layout table.*

Understanding text formatting

We can make use of two approaches for formatting text. One employs the Property Inspector panel, whilst the other uses the dedicated submenu on the main menu. Both offer similar formatting options. In our discussion here, we will make use of both approaches.

The most common attribute associated with text is the font face. We can choose from a predefined list or add new font faces. Dreamweaver 4.0 by default comes with a list of font groups, referred to as the font combination. The combination contains a number of different faces, grouped so as to improve the chances of a browser being able to display contents using a desired font face. In fact, this highlights a common difficulty whereby the chosen font for developing a site may not be available for the receiving browser. In this

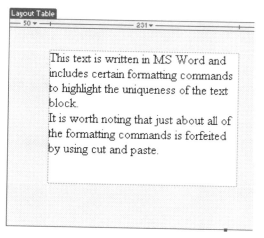

Figure 4.5 Using cut and paste to insert a text block within a page.

case, the browser will resort to using the default set of fonts. Using a combination means that the browser will display the contents with the first font face. If it does not recognize it, it will try with second. Failing that then it will continue to try the remaining until the group is exhausted. After which, it will display the contents using the default font.

To view or to change a font combination, we can use Text | Font or the Property Inspector panel. Figure 4.6 shows both cases. Within these, there is an option to add to the list. This option, as Figure 4.6 shows, is Edit Font List. If this option is chosen then we are presented with a dialogue box. The purpose of this is to facilitate the creation, modification and deletion of font combinations.

The Edit Font List dialogue box, as depicted by Figure 4.7, has a number of sections: we can choose to create a fresh combination list, to edit an existing list, to remove a list, or to re-order lists (so that when the list is displayed, a particular

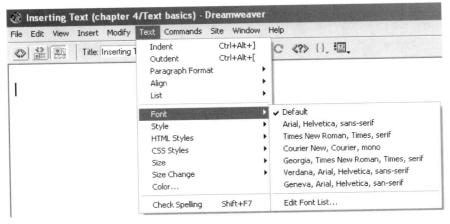

Figure 4.6 *Choosing a font combination.*

combination is at top of the list). The '+' and '-' buttons are used respectively to add or to remove a list, whilst the up and down arrows are used to re-position a highlighted combination within the list. To edit a list, we simply highlight it so that all the font faces belonging to it are displayed within the Chosen Fonts window. We can then use the double horizontal and vertical arrows to either add or remove fonts. Figure 4.8 provides an animated illustration of creating a new list. Once created, it is re-positioned so that it is listed second from the top. We can then make use of it for development like the other font combinations.

The font combinations can be applied to selected text or be chosen so that subsequent text is written using a combination. The selected text can be as small as a single character, so that characters belonging to the same word can be using different font faces. Figure 4.9 shows an example.

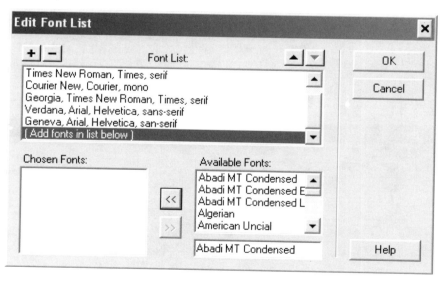

Figure 4.7 The Edit Font List dialogue box.

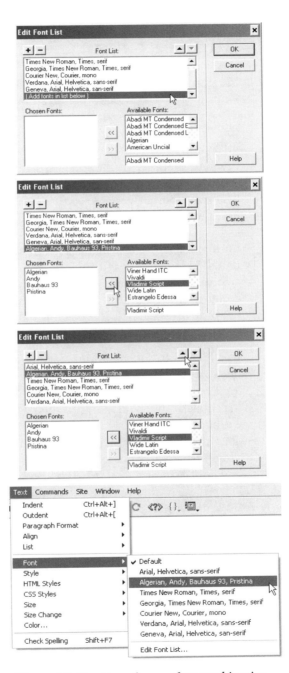

Figure 4.8 *Creation of a new font combination.*

Adjusting text size

We can change the size of selected text, whether a single character or a complete paragraph. Either choose Text | Size or use the respective pull down menu located within the Property Inspector panel to pick a desired size. Figure 4.10 shows both options. The sizes available range from 1 to 7, where 1 represents the smallest size and 7 the largest. These correlate with font sizes used in web (HTML) development. The sizes themselves are relative rather than absolute values and their appearance is connected to the actual default font size specified for a browser. Choosing either the Default option from the menu or 3 from the Property Inspector panel, best matches with the default setting of a browser. A size value of less than 3 will make the text smaller than the default, whilst a higher value will make the text bigger than the base browser size. It is often worth experimenting before deciding upon a font size.

In addition to setting a font size, we also have the option of increasing or decreasing a size. The same pull down menu on the Property Inspector panel can be used for this, or we can make use of the main menu. In this case, as Figure 4.11 shows, we choose Text | Size Change. The increments (or decrements) are with reference to the default value of 3. Therefore, if we choose +2 from the menu then this will result in a font size of 5 (3+2) being applied to the selected text. From Figure 4.11, we can see that the maximum increment of +4 will return a highest font size of 7, whilst maximum decrement of -3 will give us a font size of 0. This will in most

Figure 4.9 _Characters using different font faces._

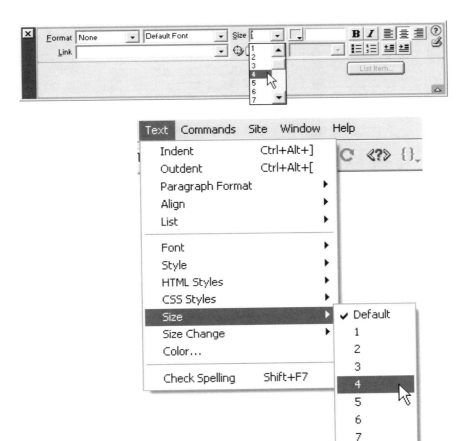

Figure 4.10 *Choosing a font size.*

browsers make the text appear as if using size 1. Going beyond the two extremes (1 and 7), in fact, does not return a bigger or smaller size than the specified range. The browser will in this case use either 1 or 7 as the font size for displaying the text.

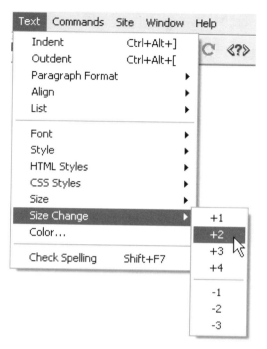

Figure 4.11 Choosing a font size addendum.

Adjusting text position

Text can also be aligned to the left, centre, or right. We can use the corresponding three buttons on the Property Inspector panel or choose Text | Align and then the desired alignment. Figure 4.12 shows the position of the three buttons on the Property Inspector panel. Both approaches will align the contents of a cell as long as the insertion cursor is present, regardless of whether any text is selected.

Next to aligning text is the option of indenting (and outdenting). Assuming text is left aligned, the indent option will shift the text towards the right. The outdent will move the text the opposite way, towards the left. This is often used to correct any unwanted indents. Two buttons on the Property

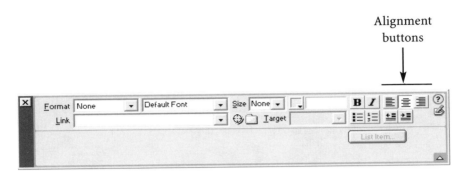

Figure 4.12 *Text alignment buttons on the Property Inspector panel.*

Inspector panel (below the text alignment options) can be used for this. Alternatively, we can choose Text | Indent or Text | Outdent to implement the same. Figure 4.13 provides an animated illustration of indent. Starting from the top image, the text is consistently indented from the left. We can view outdent as being the reverse process: starting from the bottom image, we can move towards the first image by outdenting.

Adjusting text colour

Text colour can also be modified. The text is normally written using the default colour settings. This is contained within the page properties dialogue box. As mentioned in Chapter 1, we can open this by choosing Modify | Page Properties. The resulting dialogue box is shown in Figure 4.14. We note that the default text colour is specified (in the example shown it is red). By changing this, the writing ink will change. The effect of this will be on all text that appears on the page. It will change to the default colour setting, whether it is selected or not. This may not be desirable, unless we are looking at establishing one text colour for the page.

We can, fortunately, change the colour of selected text in a number of ways – all of which overwrite the default settings. In other words, we can change the colour of a single character, a group of characters, a word, a group of words, a sentence and so on.

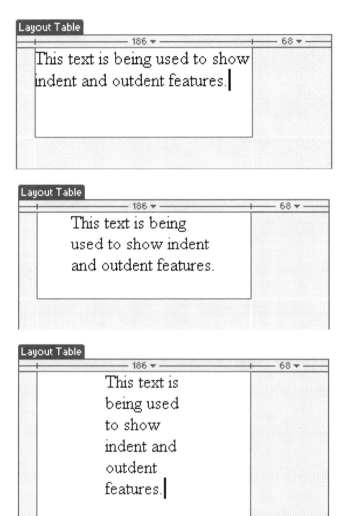

Figure 4.13 Effect of indenting text.

To change the colour of selected text, we can choose any of the following three approaches:

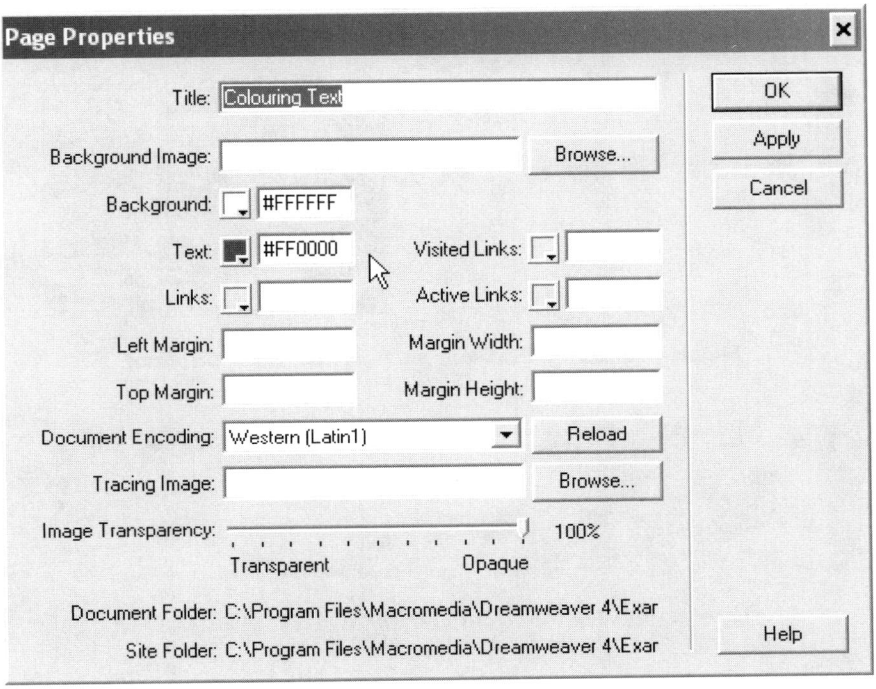

Figure 4.14 Page Properties dialogue box containing option for text colour.

- Use the colour palette located in the Property Inspector panel to select a desired colour. Figure 4.15 depicts the scenario.
- Enter a colour name or hexadecimal number in the colour entry field on the Property Inspector panel. In fact, the colour palette option (above) results in the Dreamweaver 4.0 environment automatically creating a hexadecimal number in the entry field. Figure 4.16 shows the case where blue has been entered in the entry field and the colour palette thumbnail reflecting the new entry.
- Alternatively, we can use the main menu to specify a colour. Here, choose Text | Colour to open up a respective colour dialogue box. Figure 4.17 (also Plate II) shows an illustration of the dialogue box. This opens up a number of ways to select and customize the text colour.

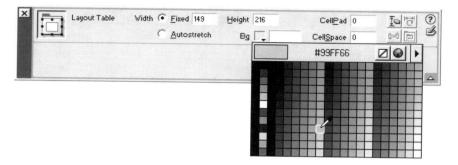

Figure 4.15 Using the colour palette to choose text colour.

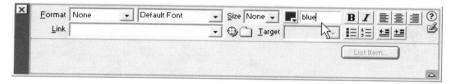

Figure 4.16 Using the colour entry field to specify text colour.

To make the text colour match the default setting, we simply remove any colours that are used by the text. To do this, select the text and then open up the colour palette within the Property Inspector panel (see Figure 4.15). By clicking the button with a white background and a diagonal red line (second button on the top right), the text colour resorts to the default setting.

Before concluding our discussion on text colours, it is worth noting that the default colour settings are part of what is referred to as the colour schema. This, in practice, means that certain colour combinations for the foreground and background work well with both browsers and more importantly with viewers. The Dreamweaver 4.0 development environment hosts a number of these colour schema. As Figure 4.18 shows, we choose Commands | Set Color Scheme to open up the corresponding dialogue box. The resulting dialogue box is shown in Figure 4.19 (also Plate II).

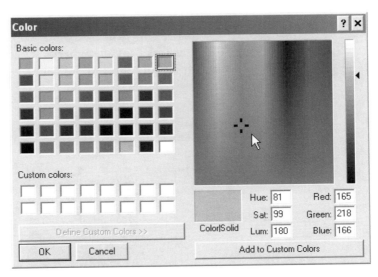

Figure 4.17 Colour dialogue box for text (also Plate II).

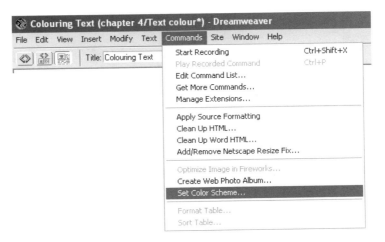

Figure 4.18 Option to choose a colour scheme.

The Set Color Scheme dialogue box has three parts. To select a new colour scheme, we choose a colour from the column headed Background. In Figure 4.19 (also Plate II), Magenta background is highlighted. The colour combinations linked to this are then shown in the second column, headed Text and

Links. We note that in this case there are three colour schemes available to us. Before applying any colour schema, the third part of the dialogue box provides a preview. Simply click on a colour scheme (first column, and then any of combinations listed in the second column) to preview.

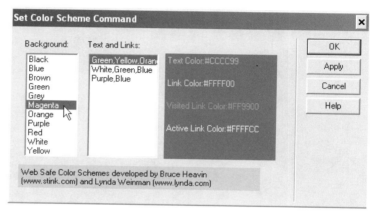

Figure 4.19 *Colour schema dialogue box (also Plate II).*

Adjusting text styling

Basic text styling (bold, italic, underline, strikethrough, and the like) is also possible. We can italicize and bold selected text through the Property Inspector panel. The two buttons are placed adjacent to the alignment options (see Figure 4.12). A fuller set of style options is available through the main menu. Choose Text | Style. Figure 4.20 depicts the scenario.

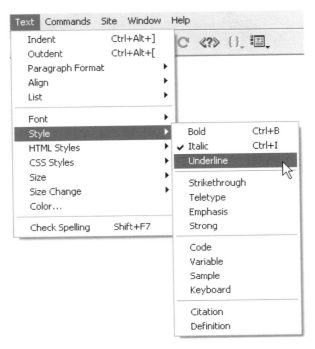

Figure 4.20 *Text styling options via* Text | Style.

Using text search

The Dreamweaver 4.0 environment includes a text search facility. This is rather comprehensive, but for the time being we can view this as being similar to the find, find and replace commands found in other word processors. To use this, choose Edit | Find and Replace. This opens the dialogue box shown in Figure 4.21. In the example shown, we want to locate the word 'world' in the current document. To quickly find the next matching word, use the function key F3.

Apart from being able to replace text words within a current document, we can also expand the search to cover the entire local site and look for specific tags. Figure 4.22

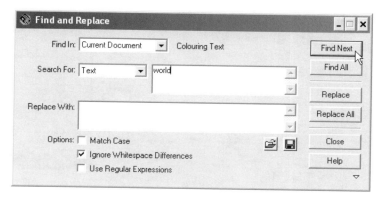

Figure 4.21 Find and replace dialogue box.

shows the contents of the pull down menus associated with the Find In and Search For parameters. Choosing a particular option changes the contents of the dialogue box. Selecting the Text (Advanced) search feature, for example, results in the dialogue box shown in Figure 4.23. The purpose of the new parameters is to specify exactly how the search should be undertaken. In other words, the constraints (if any) that should be used in the search process. If, for example, we had the following text containing some HTML tags (refer to Chapter 9 for information on HTML tags):

```
The  <b>Internet<b>  provides  a  super  way  of
interacting  with  people  on  remote  sites.
Thousands of <i>messages<i> are exchanged on the
Internet in less than a fraction of a second. The
Internet is here to stay.
```

Then a search for the word Internet will return three hits if the option to count within tags (as shown in Figure 4.23) is set. Otherwise, two hits will be recorded. The '+' and '-' buttons allow for further refinement whereby attributes associated with a tag can also be specified. Although we used a rather straightforward example to illustrate the basic working of the search method, a site containing multiple pages and thousands of words (as well as code) requires a sophisticated search facility. This is exactly what the Dreamweaver 4.0 environment offers.

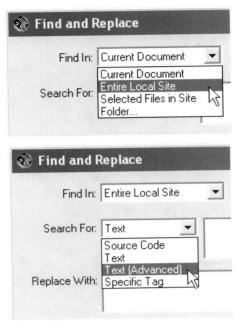

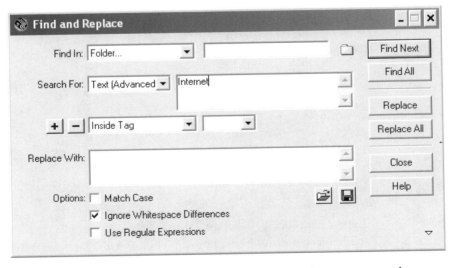

Figure 4.22 *Options within Find and Replace dialogue box.*

Figure 4.23 *Find and replace dialogue box for advance text search.*

Adding special characters

A number of characters are designated as being special since their usage has a specific place not just on web sites, but in general documents. These include the copyright symbol, the pound sign, trademark symbol and a number of others. HTML codes exist for each special character. More on HTML in Chapter 9.

To include a special character on a page (or simply to view the available characters), we can use either main menu or the Objects panel. In the case of the latter, select the Characters category as shown in Figure 4.24. This results in the panel showing a set of icons representing some common special characters. Figure 4.25 depicts the scenario. Further additional characters can be selected by choosing the Insert Other Character button. The set of characters that then become available are shown in Figure 4.26.

Figure 4.24 *Choosing Characters category for the Objects panel.*

To insert a special character using the Objects panel, position the insertion point on a page and click the icon representing the desired character. Alternatively, click and drag the icon from the panel to a desired position on the page.

Figure 4.25 Special characters icons on the Objects panel.

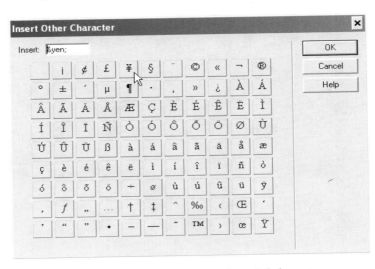

Figure 4.26 Gallery of additional special characters.

We can use the main menu to add special characters by selecting `Insert  |  Special  Characters` and then a respective character. Figure 4.27 depicts the scenario.

Figure 4.27 Using the main menu to insert a special character.

Chapter

5

Working with Images

Introduction

Text plays an important role in web development and, as seen in the previous chapter, environments such as Dreamweaver 4.0 provide a number of tools to support their insertion and modification. The primary goal being that the contents of a page need to look attractive and be informative. Pictures have, for a long time, played a critical role in presenting concepts and ideas in a compact way. Their usage for web development was hampered (particularly in the early stages) by the bandwidth restrictions imposed by the Internet. Although this still is an issue, modern technological developments have meant that not just basic graphical objects, but sophisticated elements (such as animations) are a common sight on web pages.

In this chapter, we will look at how to include images on a page, together with a set of tools that Dreamweaver 4.0 offers to facilitate working with images and optimizing them for web development.

Understanding images

A picture on a web page attracts more attention than a long essay on a particular topic. This has always been the case. The primary reason for this is that the viewing window (that is, the browser) is rectangular shaped and users are mainly reluctant to scroll up and down, or left and right, unless it is forced upon them. The second reason and most probably the main reason for acceptance (expectance) of pictures on web pages is that text (especially normal print at 10 to 12 points) is difficult and tiring to read off a screen.

Similar to text, however, pictures (or more appropriately, images) come in various formats. The format chosen to save an image depends on a number of factors including content, quality and target bandwidth for transfer. There are three formats, however, which are more commonly used than others: GIF (Graphical Interchange Format), PNG (Portable Network Group), and JPEG (Joint Photographic Experts Group). All three have clear applications in mind and just about all commercially available software packages provide support for them. The difference between the formats is mainly due to the way the images are compressed and stored. Taking JPEG as an example, it is primarily aimed at representing photographic content. Photographs, as we may know, are made from millions of small dots, each dot has its own intensity and colour. More dots and colours result in bigger file sizes. Therefore, the JPEG format allows a balance to be reached between file size on one hand and the quality of an image on the other. As we will see, Dreamweaver 4.0 works with all three graphical formats.

Adding images to a page

An image included on a web page is always a separate file, whose location is referenced within the generating HTML code. Since we can work in the design view of the Dreamweaver 4.0 environment (as mentioned in Chapter 1), we are able to create a page using the visual pictorial form. In other words, the text and images will look to be part of the same page (which is the case), but the images themselves will be contained in separate files.

The way Dreamweaver 4.0 environment works with images is very similar to that discussed for text. In fact, we could view text and image as being two objects and the environment provides tools to insert and reformat these for their inclusion on a page. We can therefore include an image directly on to the document window (or within a table) and use its associated attributes in the Property Inspector panel. More so, and as we will see, we can add behaviours to the images to create an interactive and attractive page.

Although the environment supports limited editing of images, it is not a graphical editor. As such, it lacks a number of tools normally found to create and edit images. The environment, however, does allow a preferred external editor to be attached so that when an image does need modification, the graphical editor can be invoked. To attach an external editor, select Edit | Preferences to open the corresponding dialogue box. Then choose File Types/Editors as the category. The dialogue box should look similar to that shown in Figure 5.1. Enter the path (or use browse to locate the executable application) in the text field labelled External Code Editor. Macromedia recommends that the external editor needs to be Fireworks (4.0) since it returns PNG formats by default. We can use this, or any suitable alternative, as long as the graphical editor supports image formats such as GIF, PNG, and JPEG.

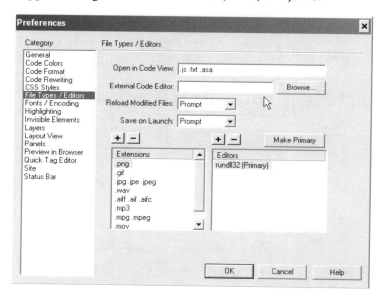

Figure 5.1 *Defining a default external editor for images.*

An image can be included by defining an insertion point (location for the image) on the page and then doing one of the following:

- Choose Insert | Image; or
- Select Insert Image button on the Objects panel. Make sure the Common category is open for the image insertion option to be available. Figure 5.2 depicts the position of the Insert Image button on the Objects panel; or
- Click Control + Alt + I keys.

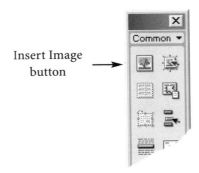

Insert Image
button →

Figure 5.2 *Position of Insert Image button on Objects panel.*

Selecting any of the above three options, opens a corresponding dialogue box. This is shown in Figure 5.3, where we note that the dialogue box has several parts to it: a list of all images residing in the selected folder is provided. A preview window is included to facilitate a quick view of any file (image) that is selected. If a preview is not available, then click on an image file and ensure that the Preview Images option is checked. The Preview Images option is located at the bottom middle of the dialogue box (see Figure 5.3).

In the example shown, the file art.png is highlighted. Below the preview window are some statistics. The resolution in pixels (500 x 500), the file type (PNG) and the file size (83) in kilobytes. An estimate of the download time (23 seconds) is also given.

Below the list of files, in Figure 5.3, are parameters relating to the selected file, name and type. The URL specifies the location of the file on the system, whilst the Relative To parameter seeks to know whether to make the image connected to the document or to the site root.

If an image file is selected and is currently not located in the current working site, the environment invokes a dialogue message. This effectively says that reference to the image file may become problematic when the site is published since the link between the source file (web page) and the image file could be lost. As such, and for efficient running of the published site, it is advizable to have all files located within the root folder. Figure 5.4 shows the respective dialogue message. Clicking on the 'Yes' button opens the file dialogue box at the current root folder and we are presented with the choice of including the image file therein.

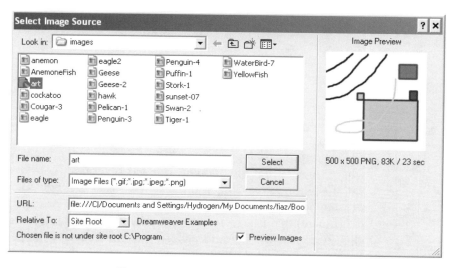

Figure 5.3 Image insertion dialogue box.

We can alternatively use the Assets panel (Window | Assets) to include an image in the web page. Recall that the Assets panel holds all files that have been used in the construction of the page to date. To use an image residing within the Assets panel, we simply click and drag the file into the document window. Figure 5.5 provides an animated illustration of this. Since the selected image forms the first component on the page, it is placed automatically at the top left corner (as discussed in Chapter 4). Alternatively, we could have inserted the image within an existing cell, similar to including a text block. The location of the insertion point on the page prior to selecting an image determines the position of the image on the web page.

We can also open the site window (Site | Site Files or Site | Site Map) and use its contents to insert images into the document window. Again, we use click and drag to select and transfer an image onto the page. Figure 5.6 shows an

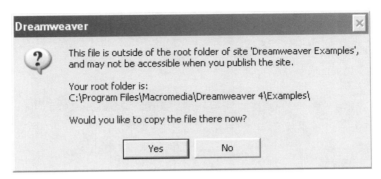

Figure 5.4 Dialogue message asking to include selected image file in root folder.

illustration of the site window for the site and the selection of the art.png image file.

The Dreamweaver 4.0 environment provides yet another way of inserting an image into a document window. This can make use of the computer desktop or a file management program such as Windows Explorer. In either case, the process of insertion is the same. If we want to transfer an image file from Windows Explorer to our page within Dreamweaver 4.0 environment, we start with having both windows open. The desired image file is then selected and dragged across to the page. The file is then included in the Dreamweaver 4.0 document window as with other approaches. In other words, the environment returns a dialogue message to say whether we want to make a copy of the image file in our root folder. The image file is then positioned at the location of the insertion point. Figure 5.7 gives an animated illustration of the scenario.

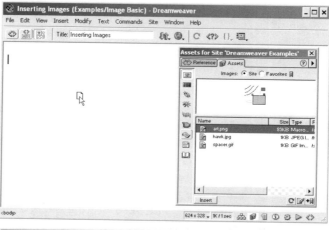

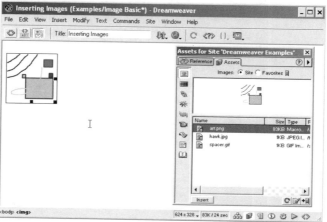

Figure 5.5 Using the Assets panel to insert an image.

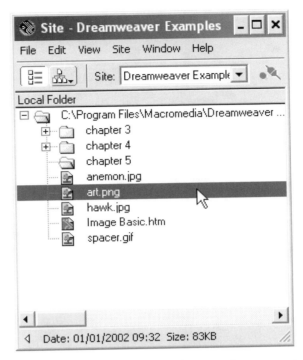

Figure 5.6 *Using the site window to insert an image on a page.*

Resizing an image

Once an image is loaded onto a page, we will normally need to customize it to match our design specifications. The primary source for modifications is through the associated Property Inspector panel. Having selected an image, we can open the panel (Window | Properties) to show the current settings. Figure 5.8 shows the Property Inspector panel for a selected image. The contents of the image file are presented as a thumbnail in the top left corner of the panel. The environment also provides additional information on the image automatically: the resolution (100 x 100), the file size (83 KB) and the file location, identified by the text field labelled as Src (source).

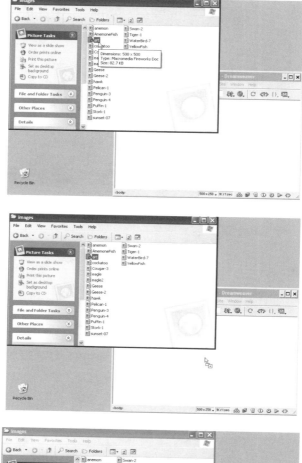

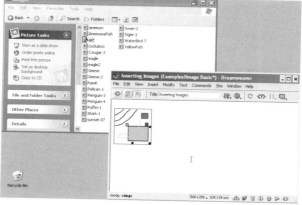

Figure 5.7 Using Windows Explorer to insert image on a page.

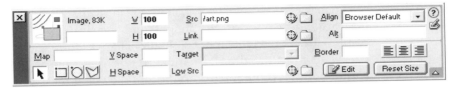

Figure 5.8 *Property Inspector panel for an image.*

We may have noticed that the display resolution is significantly less than the source image (as in the image dialogue box). The Property Inspector panel shows this to be 100 by 100, whilst the original is 500 by 500. In fact, the Dreamweaver 4.0 environment downloaded this as 500 by 500 and the height and width of the image have been reduced manually. Although the display resolution has been reduced, it does not change the file size of the image. Therefore, the download time for the image remains the same as with the original image. The image resolution (and therefore the file size) can be modified using an appropriate graphical editor such as Fireworks.

The labels W and H, therefore, respectively refer to the width and height of a selected image. This is by default expressed in pixels. Alternatively, these can be expressed as points (pt), picas (pc), millimetres (mm), centimetres (cm) and inches (in). Although as mentioned above the display resolution can be changed, we can quickly restore the original image resolution by using the Property Inspector panel: click on labels 'W' or 'H' to respectively restore original values for the image width and height. Figure 5.9 shows this, where the top image represents current settings, the middle image the restoration of the width dimension, and the bottom image the restoration of the height value. We can also make use of the Reset Size button on the Property Inspector panel. This returns both the width and height dimensions to their original values. Figure 5.10 shows the positioning of the button on the panel.

The width and height can also be adjusted interactively by using the handles associated with an image when it is selected. As Figure 5.11 shows, there are three handles: one for the width, one for the height and the third for the combination of width and height. To change dimensions, click and drag the desired handle. If the selection of the corner handle is combined with the Shift key then the aspect ratio of the image is maintained during resize. The aspect ratio of the image is the relative size of width to height.

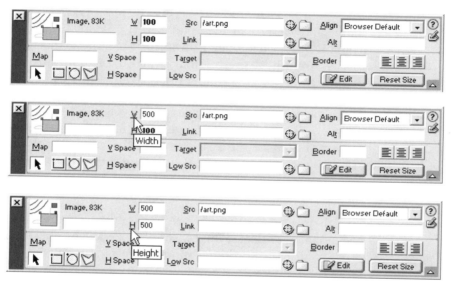

Figure 5.9 *Restoring original values for image width and height.*

If an image is placed within a cell then the cell will automatically resize to fit the image dimensions. A cell can be of bigger size than the image, however it cannot be reduced below the image size. In other words, any changes in the cell resolution will be constrained by the image or images that it contains. Interestingly enough, we are able to increase the size of an image beyond the dimensions of a cell. In this case, the cell size automatically adjusts to cover the image.

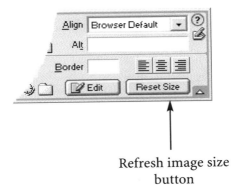

Refresh image size
button

*Figure 5.10 Restore image width and height button on the
Property Inspector panel.*

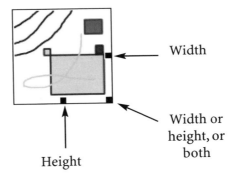

Width

Width or
height, or
both

Height

Figure 5.11 Resize handles on a selected image.

Aligning images and text

We have already encountered how to align text. Working with
images is very similar, though there are subtle differences. We
can align an image with reference to a page, or align other
objects in a desired manner to an image. Looking at the
former case first, we can align an image to the left, centre, or
to the right of a page or a table cell. Alternatively, alignment
can be made with reference to the top, middle or bottom of a
page or a cell.

To align an image or text to an image, we can make use of the main menu or the Property Inspector panel. The panel, as Figure 5.12 depicts, has a set of options for aligning an image. Table 5.1 gives a brief description of each. The best way to understand the alignment options is to develop some basic examples and to go through the options, noting their effect. As a taster for these, let us look at the last two options, Left and Right. Let us also assume that we have an image and a block of text, both of which are contained in a single cell. If Left align option is chosen then the overall effect would be to position the image to the left and the text to the right of the cell. This is shown in Figure 5.13 (also Plate III). Alternatively by selecting the Right align option, the image will be positioned next to the right edge of the cell and the text block towards the left. Figure 5.14 (also Plate III) shows this scenario. The text in both cases wraps around the image.

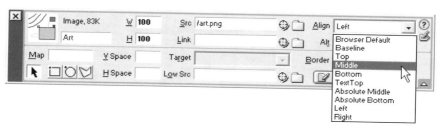

Figure 5.12 Image alignment options on Property Inspector panel.

We can also adjust the distance between an image and its surroundings. On the Property Inspector panel there are two parameters, which cater for this. The V Space parameter sets the vertical spacing in pixels, whilst the H space caters for horizontal spacing. For example, setting a V Space of 50 pixels will result in a space boundary of 50 pixels for the top and 50 pixels for the bottom edges. Likewise, specifying 30 pixels for the H Space will return 30 pixels to the right side and 30 pixels to the left of the selected image. Figure 5.15 depicts this scenario where the top figure represents the original (with no V Space or H Space), whilst the bottom figure has settings of 50 and 30 pixels respectively for V Space and H Space.

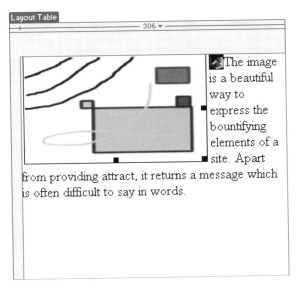

Figure 5.13 Example of Left alignment (also Plate III).

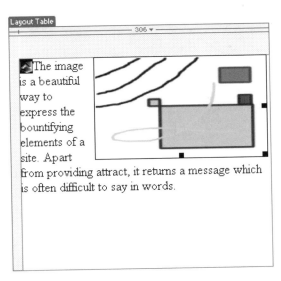

Figure 5.14 Example of Right alignment (also Plate III).

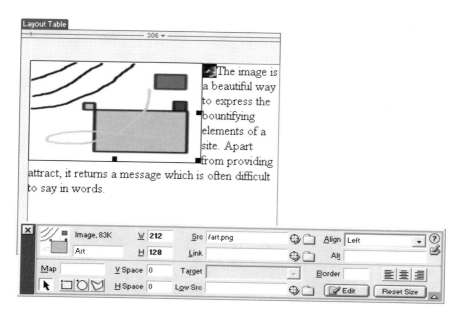

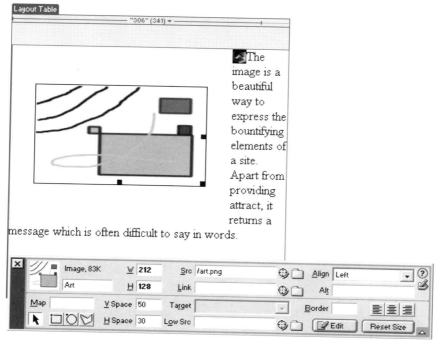

Figure 5.15 Effect of using V Space and H Space.

Table 5.1 Image alignment options.

Alignment Option	Brief Description
Browser Default	Normally baseline, but depends upon the browser settings.
Baseline	Aligns objects (text or image) with reference to lower object baseline.
Top	Aligns objects (text or image) with reference to upper object top edge.
Middle	Aligns the text baseline with the middle of a selected image.
Bottom	Similar to baseline, aligns objects to lower object baseline.
TextTop	Aligns image with reference to tallest character in text block.
Absolute Middle	Aligns objects to exact middle.
Absolute Bottom	Aligns to the absolute bottom with reference to lower object bottom edge.
Left	Aligns image to the left margin.
Right	Aligns image to the right margin.

Before concluding our discussion on alignment, it is worth noting the use of the main menu for aligning objects. We have already seen in the previous chapter (Chapter 4) the use of Text | Align options for aligning text blocks. In some cases, we can use the same options to align the contents of cells, and even the initial layout table. This provides the option of left, centre and right alignment. Choosing a cell and then opening the Property Inspector panel (either via Window | Properties or through Modify | Selection Properties) enables the contents of a cell to be aligned with reference to the four edges of the cell. In other words, we can align not just horizontally, but vertically (top, middle, bottom, and baseline). There are, therefore, a variety of ways of aligning images, with reference to other objects, or with a cell boundary.

Editing an image

We noticed earlier that an image could be edited using a preferred external editor. Dreamweaver 4.0 environment only provides minimal support for modifying an image. To invoke an external editor for a selected image, we can use the Property Inspector panel, the main menu, or the context menu. Starting with the panel, we choose the Edit button. The button is located at the bottom right half of the panel. Figure 5.16 shows the positioning of the button on the Property Inspector panel.

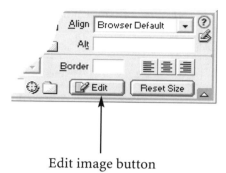

Edit image button

Figure 5.16 Edit image button on the Property Inspector panel.

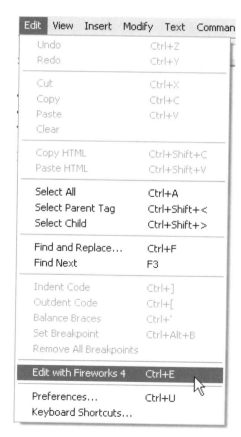

Figure 5.17 Invoking the external image editor via main menu.

Alternatively, we can make use of the main menu to open the external image editor. For this, select `Edit | Edit with Fireworks 4`. This is shown in Figure 5.17. The option to use Fireworks 4 is linked to the default editor set in the preferences dialogue box. Changing the default editor to Flash 5.0, for example, will update the option to Edit with Flash.

In addition to the two ways mentioned above, we can open an external image editor through the context menu associated with the selected image. Click on the right (mouse) button to display the menu shown in Figure 5.18. We note, similar to the main menu, this offers the option of Edit with Fireworks 4. Again, this is based on the default editor set in the preferences dialogue box. Looking more closely at Figure 5.18, we note that below the Edit with Fireworks 4 option is the choice of using another editor. The option Edit With provides for this by opening a dialogue box for browsing to a desired application program.

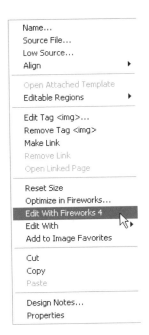

Figure 5.18 Invoking the external image editor via context menu.

When an external editor, such as Fireworks 4, is launched, it automatically opens the selected image. Any changes can be registered using the Update command within Fireworks 4 (File | Update). As Figure 5.19 (also Plate IV) shows, a Done button is made available to also transfer updates on to the Dreamweaver 4.0 environment.

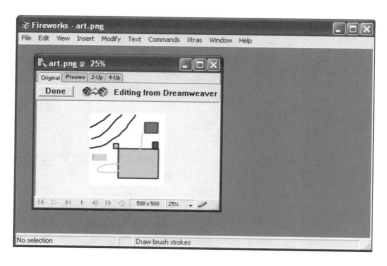

Figure 5.19 *Editing image in Fireworks 4 (also Plate IV).*

Using Alt attribute

Another feature available on the Property Inspector panel is the Alt text field. The Alt (alternative) text is a HTML attribute (see Chapter 9 for more information on working with HTML in the Dreamweaver 4.0 environment). The purpose of this is to display text instead or in addition to an image. Although most viewers will be browsing the web using graphical tools, there are browsers that do not display pictures and work only with text. In addition, the option of not displaying graphics is always available on browser settings, including modern browsers. This option is primarily there because of the download issues related to images. Viewers can thus switch off the show images option to avoid delays in downloading material across the Internet. Having to deal with text only can also assist viewers who have impaired sight. In this case, speech synthesizers can be used to audibly broadcast the contents (text information). Browsers also interpret the alternative text as a tool tip so that when a cursor is placed on top or in the vicinity of an image, a text box opens with the Alt text. Therefore, having alternative text for images can be helpful to a variety of audience.

Figure 5.20 shows the location of the Alt text field on the Property Inspector panel. The purpose of this option is to provide a brief description, rather than a title, for the selected image. The Dreamweaver 4.0 environment also keeps a track of 'missing' Alt text. In other words, images are scanned to see whether there is any alternative text associated with it. This is fed back as a report, for the designer's convenience. The report is generated through using a corresponding option on the main menu. To choose this, select Site | Reports. This opens the dialogue box shown in Figure 5.21. As this depicts there are a number of different reports, or feedback, that can be gained. We will look at generating reports in detail in Chapter 11 where the focus would be on how to test and publish a site. Figure 5.21, however, does highlight the option to generate a report on missing Alt, which can be for a particular document or the entire site. The report would contain a list of all images and highlight those with missing Alt information.

Alternative text field

Figure 5.20 Alternative text field on the Property Inspector panel.

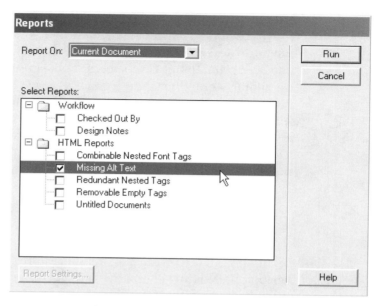

Figure 5.21   *Report generator dialogue box.*

Creating image rollover effects

We can also create rollover effects whereby an image is swapped with another when the cursor is placed over the image area. Clearly, we will need two images for this to work properly. Figure 5.22 (also Plate IV) shows two images: the image on the left is art.png and the one on the right is planets.png. Both images have been created using Fireworks 4.0. The image that is displayed as the page is loaded is referred to as the primary image, whilst the second image is called the rollover image since it appears when a cursor is placed over the image area. The two images need to be the same size; otherwise, the Dreamweaver 4.0 environment automatically adjusts the size of the rollover image to match the primary image dimensions.

To create a rollover effect, do the following:

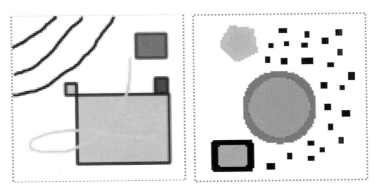

Figure 5.22 *Two images to be used for rollover effect (also Plate IV).*

- Within the document window, position the cursor (insertion point) to identify the location for the images. It is best to create a table cell and then to place the insertion point within it.
- Choose one of the following three options to insert an image for rollover effect:
  - ○ Click the Insert Rollover Image button on the Objects panel. This becomes available when the Objects panel category is set to Common. Figure 5.23 shows the positioning of the Insert Rollover Image button on the panel.
  - ○ Instead of just clicking the Insert Rollover Image button, click and drag the icon onto a cell where the rollover effect will take place. This is similar to the above option, except that the insertion point can be selected on the fly. Figure 5.24 gives an animated illustration of the process. The point to note is the changing cursor shape from a hand (on top of the Objects panel) for selection, to cannot insert shape, and finally to add shape. The latter occurs when an insertion point (such as the inside of a cell) is reached. Although in Figure 5.24 the insertion cell is the one positioned right, we could have easily moved the cursor across to the left and made this the image rollover effect cell.
  - ○ The third way to initiate the image rollover effect is through the main menu. In this case, choose Insert |

`Interactive Images` and then Rollover image. Figure 5.25 depicts the scenario.

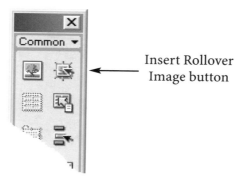

Insert Rollover
Image button

Figure 5.23 Insert rollover image button on the Objects panel.

- Selecting any of the above three options results in the opening of a corresponding dialogue box. This is shown in Figure 5.26.
- As the dialogue box shows, there are four parts:
  ○ Label the rollover image by inserting a name in the text field titled Image Name.
  ○ Type or browse path for the primary image (art.png) in the text field labelled Original Image.
  ○ Type or browse path for the rollover image (planets.png) in the text field labelled Rollover image.
  ○ Type or browse path for the file which will be executed when the rollover image is clicked. At this stage, we can leave this blank. Dreamweaver 4.0 automatically attaches a null link (shown with a # symbol) to indicate no action is required if the rollover image is clicked.
- Having left the text field labelled 'When Clicked, Go To URL' empty, we can close the Insert Rollover Image dialogue box by clicking OK.

Although we have not linked the image rollover, the null link is important and should not be deleted, as this will impair the image rollover effect. The Property Inspector panel has a text field to show any links of the selected image. In this case, as Figure 5.27 shows, a null link (#) is displayed. More on links in the next chapter (Chapter 6).

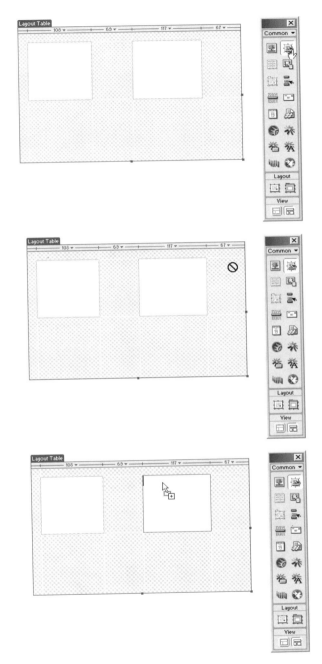

Figure 5.24 *Click and drag rollover image to desired table cell.*

What we have just done is to create an image rollover effect. The primary image is art.png and the rollover image is planets.png. Within the dialogue box (see Figure 5.26), there is an option to preload images. The goal of this option is to ensure smooth rollover effects as we move from primary to rollover images. In other words, minimal delay (if any) is experienced between the swapping of images. Check the 'Preload Rollover Image' box so that both images are downloaded to the browser cache to ensure faster displays.

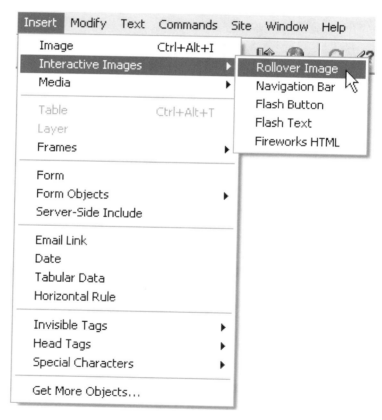

Figure 5.25 Using the main menu to initiate image rollover effect.

To view the rollover effect, press function key F12 to launch the default browser. This should display the primary image

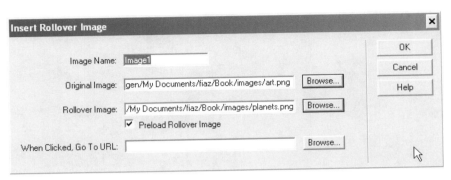

Figure 5.26 Insert rollover image dialogue box.

Null link
symbol (#)

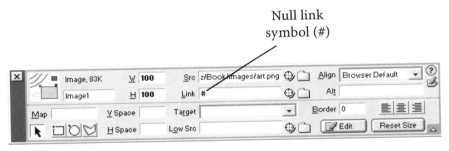

Figure 5.27 Null link (#) is displayed for the image rollover.

and then swap to the rollover image when the mouse cursor is placed on top of it. As Figure 5.28 (also Plate V) depicts, the browser first displays the art.png image and as the mouse cursor is positioned close to this, then the planets.png image is shown.

We have activated the rollover effect by using mouse over property. In other words, the images swap when the mouse goes over the primary image. There are other ways of activating such events (for example, mouse clicking, mouse off, etc). These come under the broad heading of behaviours. We will look at some of these in subsequent chapters.

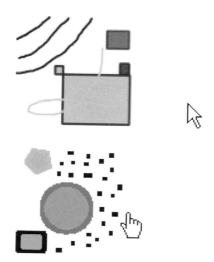

Figure 5.28 Rollover effect displayed in a browser (also Plate V).

Adding a background image

A web page often has a background to reflect a business or product identity. The Dreamweaver 4.0 environment supports this by providing a simple way of including background images to a page. To include a background image, choose Modify | Page Properties. As Figure 5.29 shows, the corresponding dialogue box that opens contains a number of options for customizing the page properties. This includes the option of adding a background image: we can type in the path or browse for a file containing the desired background image. Having specified the file, we can then use the Apply button to view how the background will look, or simply choose OK for confirmation. An example of how a background image may look on a page is shown in Figure 5.30 (also Plate V). It can be seen that the image is tiled to fit the page. The number of tiles used is a factor of the image resolution, as well as the resolution of the document window. We can control the number and the manner in which tiles appear on a page using cascading style sheets. Although style sheets are discussed in Chapter 10, it is worth noting that through applying a style sheet to a page we can constrain the background image to appear once only on a page, or to tile vertically only or horizontally only.

The use of a background image should correlate well with the contents of a page. In some cases, text on a page may be difficult to read on a tiled image background. In such circumstances, a background colour for the text will be required. If the text were within a cell, then a background colour for the cell would suffice.

Background image
text field

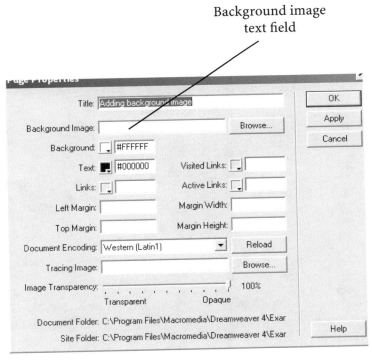

Figure 5.29 Adding a background image to a page.

Adding an image border

An image can be framed through using the border attribute. The border attribute, as depicted in Figure 5.31, is located on

Figure 5.30 Background image on a page (also Plate V).

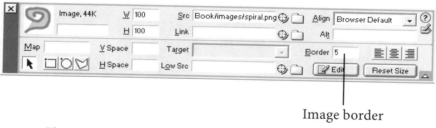

Image border

Figure 5.31 Image border attribute on Property Inspector panel.

the Property Inspector panel. The border size is specified in pixels for a selected image. Figure 5.32 shows an example of where an image has been framed using a border of five pixels. Clearly, to return to a borderless image, we simply enter zero pixels as the border size.

Looking at the Property Inspector panel, we note that it does not contain an option for colouring the border. One way of achieving this is to select the image and then to choose Modify | Page Properties. An option to set the colour of the text is provided (see Figure 5.29). This is labelled as Text. Although this sets the text colour, since we have the image selected, it will also change the border colour. Choose a desired colour and press OK. The text colour will also change, but we can reset this using the Property Inspector panel.

Figure 5.32 Adding a border to an image.

Chapter 6

Working with Links and Hyperlinks

Introduction

The attraction of the Internet and, more precisely, that of the World Wide Web is the implementation of hyper information. That is, the attachment of information sources which could reside within a page, or on a local site, or even be external to the current site. A web site consists of a number of pages so that hyperlinks facilitate navigation between pages. The term hypertext is used to describe a text which contains an embedded reference to another information source. Extending this concept to images, sound, video, etc, leads to hypermedia. A hyperlink in this sense simply means that a link exists between the source (for example, some words, or an image) and the embedded reference (for example, another section of the page, or remote site). Hyperlinks have a common place in web site development, though at times they add to the fuzziness of knowing exactly where one is when browsing cross sites.

We have seen how to layout a page, include text and images, modify and edit contents. In this chapter, we will explore the variety of ways of including links to the contents. This will include a discussion on defining paths, using images for linking, as well making text hyper and adding mailto links.

Defining link paths

Before looking at ways to include hyperlinks, it is important that we understand the way paths connecting to a linked destination can be defined. There are two ways of describing a path, either through absolute addressing or via relative addressing. The former gives the full address, starting with the root folder. The latter provides an address with reference to the current location of a file. The best way to understand the difference is to look at an example. Figure 6.1 shows a site map for a company specializing in computer products. The company produces computers of various specifications and categorizes these into three groups: Series A, Series B, and Series C. In Figure 6.1, the folders represent the three categories and a description of each of the products is within the respective HTML files. Furthermore, the company (GoComputer PLC) folder is located within the X drive on the local system.

Let us assume that we are currently within the file Gamer.htm under the Series B folder and we wish to create a link to the file Performer.htm located in the Series C folder. To specify the path to the Performer.htm file, we can either use absolute or relative addressing. Table 6.1 shows the variants for both cases. From this, it can be seen that an absolute path commences with the root folder, whilst the relative path is with reference to the current location. The two dots and forward slash (../) is a common feature within Unix and DOS environments and means to go one level above the current position. In the example shown, this would be from the Series B to GoComputers PLC folder.

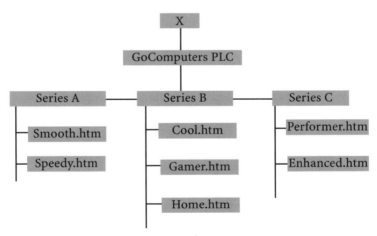

Figure 6.1 *Site structure for a computer company.*

Table 6.1 Absolute and relative addressing modes.

Address mode	Address
Absolute	X/GoComputer PLC/Series C/Performer.html
Relative	../Series C/Performer.html

So, how does this discussion assist in the development of a site? The key to this lies in understanding that absolute paths are ideal for creating links to external, remote, sites. Linking to local files and folders should always be undertaken using relative addressing. In the Dreamweaver 4.0 environment, the term document relative path is used for this. The benefit of using relative paths is that it makes a site portable since it does not require a full address – especially reference to a local system hard drive.

We, therefore, use the complete URL (Universal Resource Locator) to reference external sites and relative paths to link to local information. Dreamweaver 4.0 environment typically expresses an absolute address to a file on a local storage device as:

```
File:///X|/GoComputers PLC/Series C/Performer.htm
```

We note that this refers to the hard drive X, which may not exist when the file is published on a server. Therefore, such references need to be translated to relative paths to ensure that the developed web site works properly. We should also note that the Dreamweaver 4.0 environment initially works with absolute addresses until it is in a position to calculate the relative paths. Absolute addresses are automatically changed to relative paths when a file is saved.

In addition, the Dreamweaver 4.0 environment supports a third type of addressing. This is termed root relative paths. As the name suggests, all links in this case are with reference to the root folder, which is established by the location of the local site. The central audience for using this feature would be a comparably large web site that makes use of several servers, or a single server hosting a number of different sites.

A root relative path begins with a forward slash (/), which represents the site root folder. An example of this is as follows:

```
/stadiums/London/Wembley.htm
```

The subfolder `stadiums` (and then `London`) is placed under the root folder and the file (`wembley.htm`) is addressed using root relative path. One difficulty with using this addressing mode is that preview of pages can only take place when the site is uploaded onto a server. For our discussion here, we will work with absolute and document relative paths.

Creating linked images

In the previous chapter (Chapter 5), we looked at inserting images on a page and touched on developing an image rollover effect. We can take this further to include a linked image. In its basic form, we attach a file to the image so that when the image is activated, the linked file opens. To do this, we make use of the Property Inspector panel and the Link parameter therein. Figure 6.2 shows the position of the Link parameter on the panel. This, in fact, shows three different ways of inserting a hyperlink to the selected image:

- Type the path (URL) in the text field; or
- Use the folder icon next to the text field to browse for a file; or
- Link to a file using the point-to-file icon located next to the text field. For this to work, we need to have the Site window open (Site | Site Files). Then click on the point-to-file icon and drag out a line. The line represents the link. Drop the line on top of the file to be linked to the image. The corresponding relative address appears in the Link text field. Figure 6.3 (also Plate VI) shows an animated illustration of this. In the example shown, the selected image is linked to another image, tree.png. The effect of this, as Figure 6.4 (also Plate VII) depicts, is similar to the image rollover scenario whereby the primary image is swapped with the rollover image when the mouse is clicked over the image area.

Link image text field

Figure 6.2 Image link option on the Property Inspector panel.

Essential Dreamweaver 4.0 *fast*

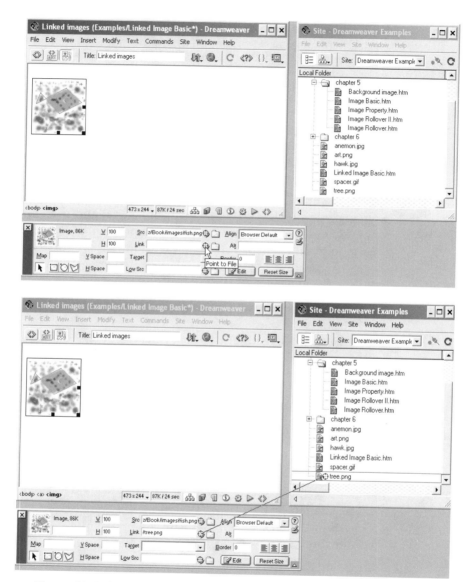

Figure 6.3 *Using point-to-file icon to create a linked image (also Plate VI).*

A border around the image can also be included, as discussed in the previous chapter, by using the Border parameter located on the Property Inspector panel. This, however, will only frame the primary image and not the linked image.

Although the example shown in Figure 6.4 (also Plate VII) appears to return a image rollover effect, it actually is returning a linked image. The image rollover process, as mentioned in the previous section, changes images as the mouse cursor goes over the image area rather than when the mouse button is clicked. In addition, the main purpose of the image rollover is to show that the mouse is over an area that when clicked will activate a linked file. In other words, we need a third file for a rollover effect: one that is displayed as the browser opens the page, the second for rollover effect, and the third when the mouse button, for example, is clicked.

To add a linked file or URL to the rollover image, we choose Insert | Interactive Images and then Rollover Image. This, as discussed in Chapter 5, opens up the dialogue box shown in Figure 6.5. This time, we can add a URL or file path to the parameter labelled 'When Clicked, Go To URL'. In the example shown in Figure 6.5, the URL www.macromedia.com has been added. Interesting enough, since we are working with an image rollover effect rather than linked image, the Property Inspector panel has the URL

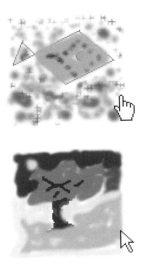

Figure 6.4 Effect of linking an image to another image is equivalent to creating a image rollover effect (also Plate VII).

address in the Link box. The rollover image path does not appear on the panel. Figure 6.6 highlights this fact.

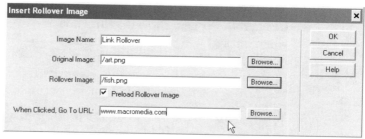

Figure 6.5 *Adding a link to an image rollover effect.*

Figure 6.6 *Property Inspector panel shows image link URL.*

Understanding image maps

The discussion in the previous section has shown how to create a linked image, where the whole area covered by an image can be used to activate a link. It is possible to work with a subset of the image and to link each subset separately. If, for example, an image represented a road map showing the routes between cities and towns, we could create subsets for each city or town so that when selected, more information on the city or town will appear. In web design terminology, the subsets are referred to as hotspots, whilst an image (like the road map) containing hotspots is called an image map. Therefore, by clicking on a hotspot, a file opens. The file could be resident locally, or be a remote (web) site.

Image maps are a common feature in web design and development and, as such, it comes as no surprise to find that software application programs such as Fireworks and Illustrator have tools to create these. Image maps can be created on the client (browser) side or on the server side. We will look at client side image maps since they are self-containing in that hyperlink information is embedded within the defining HTML document. In the case of server side image maps, hyperlink information is stored in a separate file. Client side image maps provide faster rendering and are given priority by browsers where both types of image maps are included in a document.

We start the process of creating an image map by firstly selecting an image whose area we intend to subdivide into hotspots. We then make use of the corresponding tools available on the Property Inspector panel. As Figure 6.7 depicts, there are three shape tools available to create a hotspot; namely, a rectangle, a circle and a polygon tool. There is also a text box, labelled Map, which must be completed to identify the image map. The name needs to be unique for a given page. The environment will automatically create an image name if no entry is made in the Map text box. The pointer arrow tool provides a way of selecting an image map. Once selected, an image map can be moved and resized.

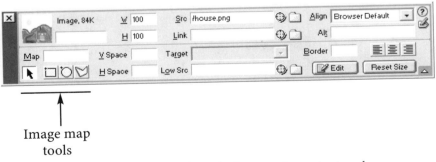

Image map tools

Figure 6.7 *Image tools on the Property Inspector panel.*

Adding image maps

We will create some hotspots for the image shown in Figure 6.8 (also Plate VII). The image consists of a house, a river, mountains and a sun. Each of these components will be used as a hotpot (hyperlinked to a specified destination address). To create a hotspot, we need to follow the steps listed below:

- Select an image (in our case the image shown in Figure 6.8).
- Open the Property Inspector panel (`Window | Properties`).
- Enter a name for the image map in the Map text box. Ensure the name is different than other names given to hotspots residing on the same page.
- Choose a selection (rectangle, circle, or polygon) tool to create a hotspot. Discussion on how to use each tool is given below.
- Once a hotspot is created, the Dreamweaver 4.0 environment automatically changes the Property Inspector panel to show the relevant attributes for the hotspot. Figure 6.9 depicts the hotspot panel.
- We can add a link path for the file or URL which will open when the hotspot is clicked. Type the relevant path in the Link text box, or click on the folder icon to locate a file or use the point-to-file icon to link the hotspot to a relevant file.
- In addition, we can add alternative text to the hotspot. This works in a similar way to the image case discussed in Chapter 4. Add the desired text in the Alt text box.
- The Target parameter specifies how and where the linked file should open (for example, in a separate window).
- Additional hotspots for an image can be created through choosing a selection tool and repeating the above steps thereafter.
- Click anywhere outside the image to apply the hotspot. This action also restores the contents of the Property Inspector panel.
- Press F12 or `File | Preview in Browser` and then the

default browser (iexplore for Microsoft Internet Explorer) to test the working of the hotspots.

We will begin at developing image maps for the image shown in Figure 6.8 by creating a hotspot for the house through the rectangle tool: select the image and then choose the rectangle tool from the Property Inspector panel. The cursor changes from an insertion to crosshair shape as it is moved across the image. Place the crosshair to the top left of the house and click and drag it diagonally across to form a rectangle to cover the whole house. On release of the mouse button, a hashed filled rectangle is drawn on top of the house. Figure 6.10 (also Plate VIII) gives an animated illustration of this. As this shows, three handles are attached to the drawn rectangle, which allow for resizing of the image map. If we wanted to make use of this (in other words, to resize), click on the pointer tool and then choose a handle to modify the dimensions of the image map.

If an image map (for example, hashed filled rectangle) is not displayed on the image, then we will need to switch this on. Select View | Visual Aids and then Image Maps to toggle the display. As Figure 6.11 depicts, we should see a tick (✓) next to the Image Maps option.

Figure 6.8 Image used to illustrate working with hotspots (also Plate VII).

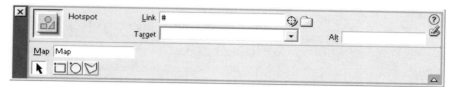

Figure 6.9 *Hotspot attributes on the Property Inspector panel.*

Once the image map is drawn, we can use the resulting hotspot Property Inspector panel to add a hyperlink to the house (www.property.com) and a brief description of the hotspot in Alt box. Figure 6.12 shows the panel with the mentioned details entered. The working of the hotspot is shown in Figure 6.13 (also Plate VIII). The hand shaped cursor is well known to depict a hyperlink and, in this case, a mouse click will result in the browser locating the linked URL. The hand shaped cursor appears only over the drawn rectangle hotspot and the contents of the Alt box are returned as a tool tip.

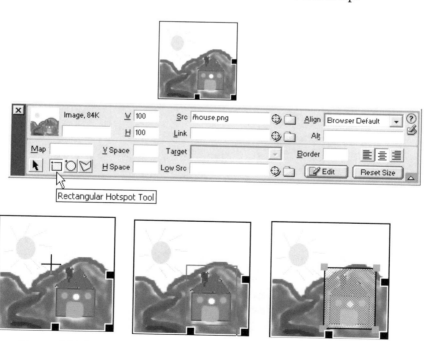

Figure 6.10 *Rectangular tool being used to create a hotspot for the house (also Plate VIII).*

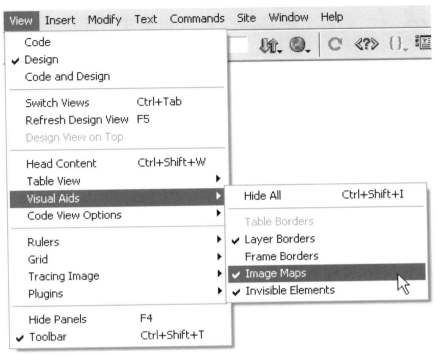

Figure 6.11 Toggling the display of image maps.

Using a similar approach, we choose the circle tool to create a hotspot for the sun. Figure 6.14 depicts the scenario where we note that the circle hotspot is selected and a hyperlink (www.sun.com) has been added. The Alt box, in addition, has some relevant text to indicate what will happen when the sun hotspot is clicked.

Next, we want to develop an image map for the river and for the mountains. We could choose to use a single map for both or a map each for the two components. Let us assume that we want to go for the latter. The process for creating an image map for the river or for the mountains is the same in that we will use the polygon tool to generate the hotspot. In our discussion here, we will develop an image map for the river.

Having selected the polygon tool from the Property Inspector panel, position the crosshair at one end of the river. Click to identify the starting point for the polygon. Then

Figure 6.12 Hotspot Property Inspector panel for the house.

Figure 6.13 Hotspot over the house (also Plate VIII).

either go clockwise or counter clockwise and click at points where the river shape changes rapidly. Each click is recognized as an endpoint to a line and defines the respective edge(s) to the polygon. In other words, after an initial click (point) additional points on the polygon are defined using further mouse clicks. These in turn reflect the changes in the shape outline.

In the case of developing an image map for the river, we go down one side of the river in a sequence and insert points at the appropriate place. Figure 6.15 (also Plate IX) shows the effect of doing this. At this stage, the polygon does not cover the river since we have not defined the width (that is, the shape) of the river. If we continue going clockwise around the river (placing the polygon points on the other side), we end up with an image map covering the whole of the river. Figure 6.16 (also Plate IX) depicts the scenario.

It takes some practice in placing the points and as such, it is wise to fine-tune the initial image map by selecting the pointer tool and adjusting the polygon points. In the worst

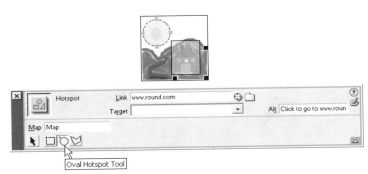

Figure 6.14 Insertion of a circle hotspot for the sun.

case, we can select and delete the image map and start again. The rule of thumb is to insert more polygon points where the shape changes are occurring. This way the polygon is following the shape outline. Alternatively, we could develop a more coarse image map that simply places the river (or the mountains) within it, without taking note of the shape contours. The exact approach very much depends on the end goal and requirements that need to be met.

Having established the image map, we then use the respective hotspot Property Inspector panel to insert a corresponding hyperlink and alternative text. The alternative text becomes more and more important as an image begins to have more hotspots. As implied in Figure 6.16 (also Plate IX), image maps tend to overlap so that when viewed in a browser, the alternative text needs to assist the viewer in choosing the desired hotspot.

Adjusting image hotspots

In the previous section, we created some image maps as a means of facilitating hyperlinks to external web sites. We noticed that image maps could be created and then edited to realize a desired shape. There are other options available to us. These include selection of multiple hotspots, setting the order of display of two or more hotspots, and aligning hotspots.

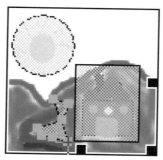

Figure 6.15 *Insertion of polygon points on one side of the river (also Plate IX).*

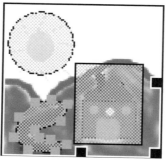

Figure 6.16 *Image map for the river (also Plate IX).*

To select more than one hotspot at a time, ensure the pointer tool on the Property Inspector panel is selected. Then, using the Shift key, click on the hotspots to be selected. Alternatively, we can choose all the hotspots belonging to an image: select the image and then use the key combination of control (Ctrl) and A.

As mentioned above, working with a number of hotspots for an image can lead to some fuzziness in terms of which hotspot is active at any one moment in time. This is particularly true for hotspots that overlap. In this case, we need to establish a display priority for the hotspots. To do this, we can make use of the main menu or the context menu. With the former, select a hotspot and then choose Modify | Arrange. This, as Figure 6.17 depicts, opens up a submenu

Figure 6.17 Setting display priority for a selected hotspot.

with the option of either sending the hotspot to the back (lowest priority) or of bringing it to the front (highest priority).

Similar options are available through the context menu. Select the image and then click on the right mouse button to open the context menu. As Figure 6.18 shows, we can choose an appropriate option from the menu.

Although the need for ordering image hotspots could be for unwanted overlap of image maps, there are occasions where such a situation may be desirable. For example, we may have the image shown in Figure 6.19 (also Plate X). Here, there are two regions: one, green for Go and the other red for Stop. Two corresponding hotspots are required. We probably start with using a rectangle tool to generate the image map for the Go region and then the circle tool for the Stop area. The result will look similar to Figure 6.20 (also Plate X).

Figure 6.18 *Establishing display order for a selected hotspot through the context menu.*

One difficulty that we may encounter is that once the circle hotspot has been created, it is not possible to select it. This is because the image map that is created first (the rectangular shape in our example) will be taken as being on top. Therefore, if we wanted to adjust the shape or position of the circular image map, we will need to take one of the following two steps:

- Select the rectangular image map and then choose Send to Back from the Modify | Arrange submenu; or
- Select the rectangular image map and then drag it across until the circular image map becomes visible. Figure 6.21 (also Plate X) depicts the scenario.

Figure 6.19 *Image with two regions: Go and Stop (also Plate X).*

Figure 6.20 *Two image maps for the respective regions (also Plate X).*

Figure 6.21 *Dragging the rectangular image map to make visible the circular image map (also Plate X).*

Although an image map can be moved interactively by clicking and dragging, we can also use the keyboard to make horizontal or vertical shifts. To do this, select an image map and use the arrow keys to move one pixel in the desired direction. Alternatively, we could do the same but this time combine it with the Shift key. This makes the increments 10 pixels rather than one.

Image maps can in addition be aligned. The possible alignments are similar to other objects in that two or more image maps can be aligned to the left, centre, right, or bottom. The main menu or the context menu can be used for this purpose. In the case of the former, choose Modify | Align and then the desired alignment (for the selected image maps) from the submenu. Figure 6.22 depicts the scenario. Alternatively, as Figure 6.23 shows, the context menu can be used to perform the same.

In addition to the alignment options, we can also use the Make Same Width and Make Same Height to resize image maps and to add some consistency to a design. These options become available when two or more image maps are selected. As shown by Figures 6.22 and 6.23, both options can be chosen using the main menu or the context menu.

An example of where these options could assist us is when a menu is being designed. Figure 6.24 shows a typical scenario, together with corresponding image maps covering each of the six choices. The image maps are all of different sizes (reflecting the word length for each menu choice) and not

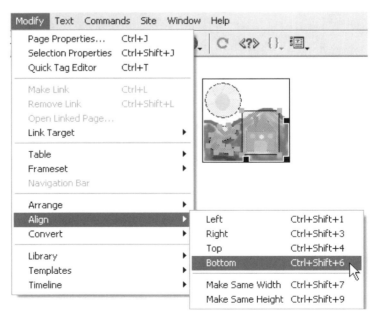

Figure 6.22 *Aligning selected image maps using the main menu.*

aligned (though the choices themselves are left justified). Using such a menu with the resulting hotspots is possible, though it will lack consistency of presentation and feel for the options. As such, the menu could be said to be short on conformity. A better way to present the menu would be to make the height and width of the image maps the same and to align all the hotspots to the left. We, therefore, undertake this requirement by firstly selecting all the image maps by using the key combination Ctrl and A. Next, the above mentioned approaches are used to adjust the image hotspots so that they have the same width and height, and are aligned to the left as desired. The result of this is shown in Figure 6.25 (also Plate XI), where clicking a choice will open up a relevant page.

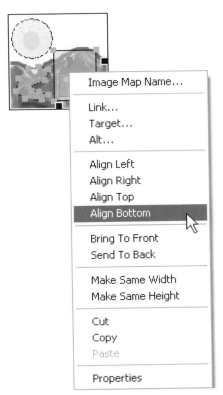

Figure 6.23 *Aligning selected image maps via the context menu.*

Linking within a page

One common requirement in web development is for a viewer to be able to move quickly to different parts of a page. Typically, this is where more information on a topic is provided. This is the case where a page is subdivided into sections and a main menu at the top of the page is provided to navigate to a desired section.

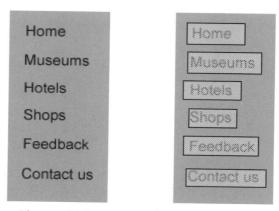

Figure 6.24 Image maps for six menu choices.

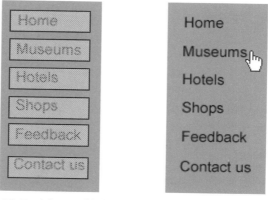

Figure 6.25 Resizing and left align the menu options (also Plate XI).

Alternatively, an embedded link could be employed to move around a page. An embedded link is where some text is set up to provide a link to a designated part of a page. We have often seen these in websites where a word or two is shown in colour (non-black) to distinguish it from rest of the text.

To generate a link within a document, we make use of the Property Inspector panel and named anchors. Anchors in general are reference points and a named anchor is, therefore, one which has a label attached to it. By placing the named anchors at desired locations on a page (for example, at the top of a page), we can link other parts of a document to it. In other words, the named anchor becomes the destination point to a hyperlink attached to it.

To create a link within a page, therefore, we need firstly to establish named anchors and then to generate the corresponding links. There are several ways of generating named anchors:

- Position the insertion point at the place on the page where the named anchor is to be included.
- Next, we need to insert the named anchor. There are three possible ways of doing this: one approach makes use of the main menu, the other Objects panel and the third, shortkeys. The way the three can be invoked is as follows:
  - Choose Insert | Invisible Tags and then Named Anchor from the submenu. Figure 6.26 depicts the scenario.
  - Alternatively, we can make use of the Objects panel by choosing the Invisibles category. Figure 6.27 depicts the scenario. The category consists of three options. Choose the named anchor icon. This is shown in Figure 6.28. In fact, if the insertion point has already been placed on the page then click on the icon. Otherwise, click and drag the icon onto the page. Figure 6.29 shows how this approach could be used to identify the location for a named location.
  - The shortkey combination for inserting a named anchor is Ctrl + Alt + A.

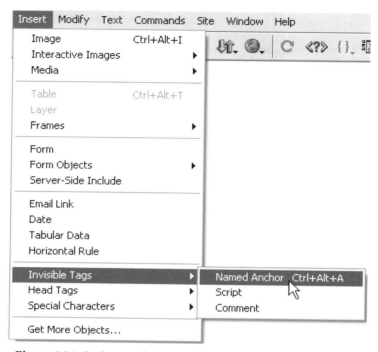

Figure 6.26 Option on the main menu to insert a named anchor.

- Selecting any one of the above three options results in the dialogue box shown in Figure 6.30. Here, we type in the name of the anchor in the text field that is provided. The name should not contain any spaces. The names are also case sensitive.

- Depending upon the environment settings, the message box shown in Figure 6.31 may appear once an anchor has been named. The message is highlighting the fact that a marker appears next to the insertion point to show that a named anchor has been inserted. The appearance of the marker is controlled by a corresponding option which acts as a toggle to show or not show what Dreamweaver 4.0 environment refers to as invisible elements. As Figure 6.32 depicts, click on View | Visual Aids and then check the Invisible Elements. A tick appears next to the selected option to say that invisible elements (such as named anchors) are to be displayed. The full set of

Figure 3.25 Basic page with content in Standard view.

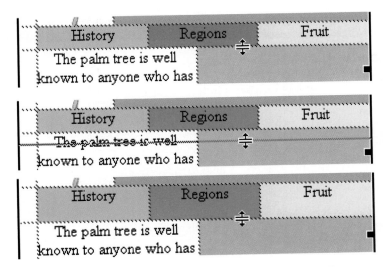

Figure 3.26 Increasing the row (menu options) height.

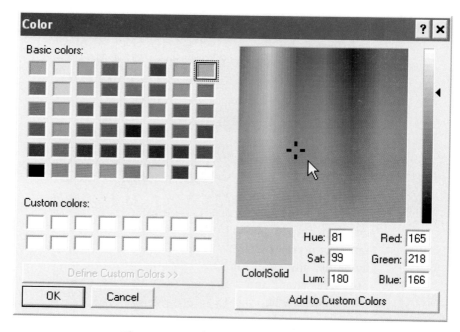

Figure 4.17 Colour dialogue box for text.

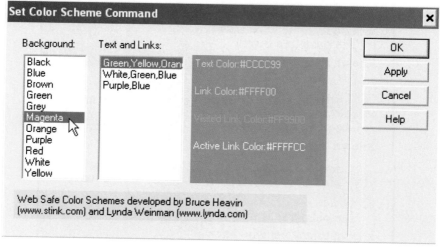

Figure 4.19 Colour schema dialogue box.

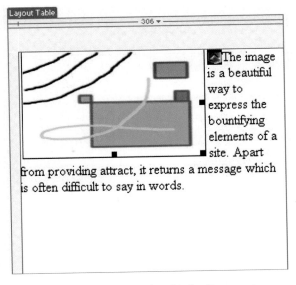

Figure 5.13 Example of Left alignment.

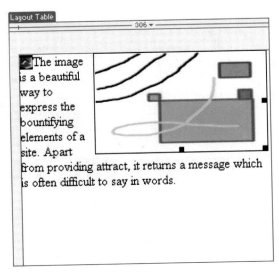

Figure 5.14 Example of Right alignment.

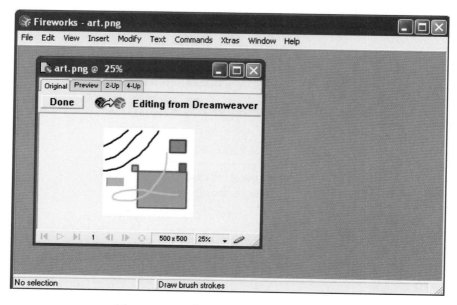

Figure 5.19 *Editing image in Fireworks 4.*

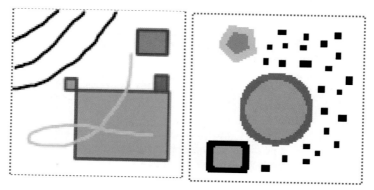

Figure 5.22 *Two images to be used for rollover effect.*

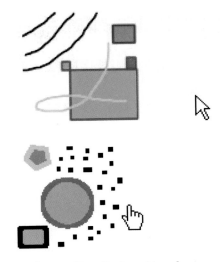

Figure 5.28 Rollover effect displayed in a browser.

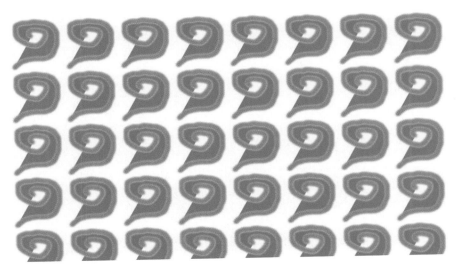

Figure 5.30 Background image on a page.

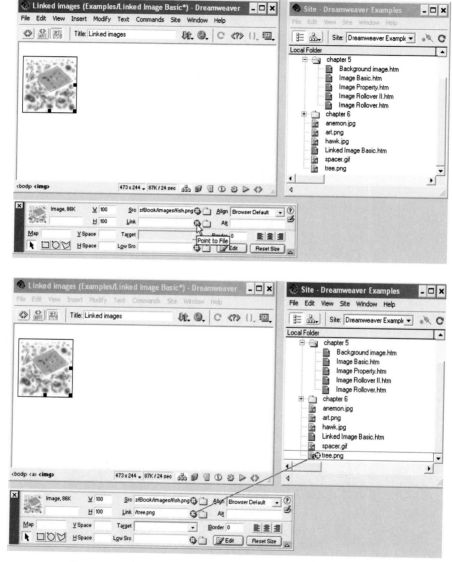

Figure 6.3 Using point-to-file icon to create a linked image.

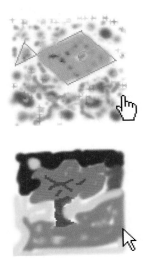

Figure 6.4 *Effect of linking an image to another image is equivalent to creating a image rollover effect.*

Figure 6.8 *Image used to illustrate working with hotspots.*

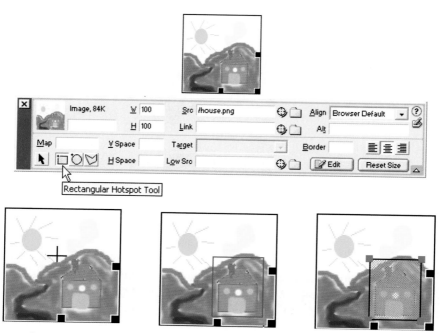

Figure 6.10 Rectangular tool being used to create a hotspot for the house.

Figure 6.13 Hotspot over the house.

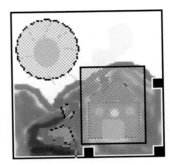

Figure 6.15 *Insertion of polygon points on one side of the river.*

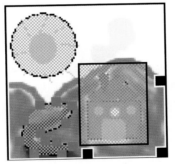

Figure 6.16 *Image map for the river.*

Figure 6.19   *Image with two regions: Go and Stop.*

Figure 6.20   *Two image maps for the respective regions.*

Figure 6.21   *Dragging the rectangular image map to make visible the circular image map.*

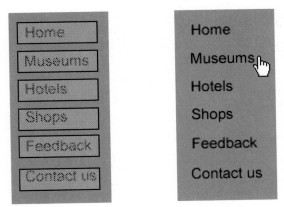

Figure 6.25 *Resizing and left align the menu options.*

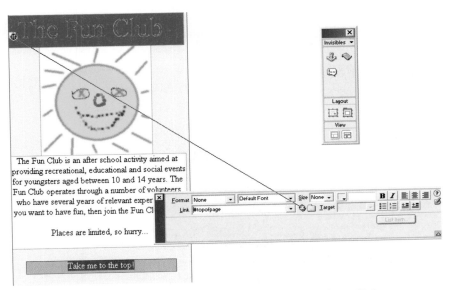

Figure 6.36 *Using point-to-file icon to create a hyperlink.*

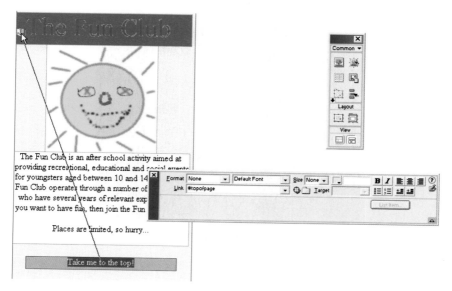

Figure 6.37 *Using Shift + drag to create a hyperlink.*

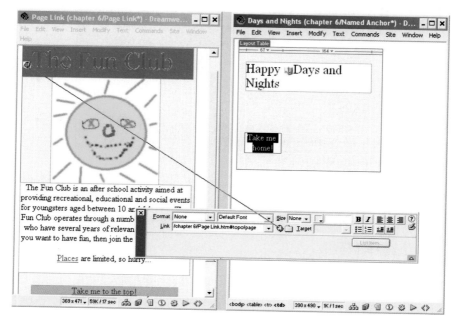

Figure 6.38 *Creating a hyperlink between two pages (files).*

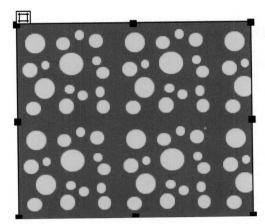

Figure 7.19 Adding a background image to a layer.

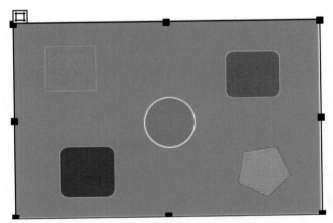

Figure 7.21 Layer containing an image to be clipped.

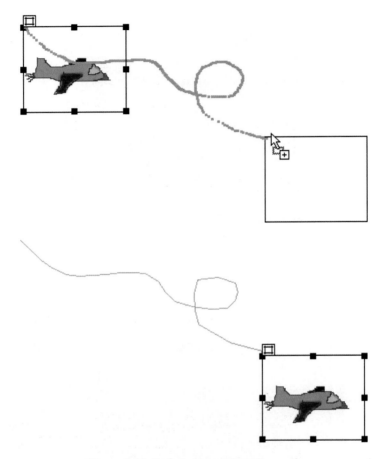

Figure 7.44 Defining an animation path.

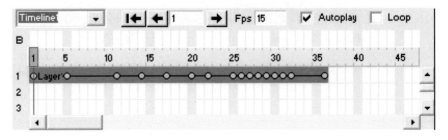

Figure 7.45 Animation bar on the timelines panel.

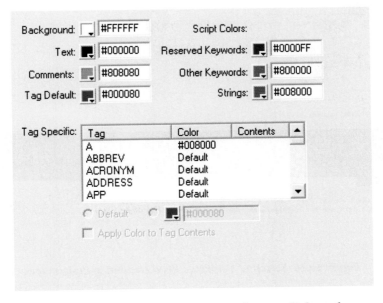

Figure 9.21 Code colour settings on preferences dialogue box.

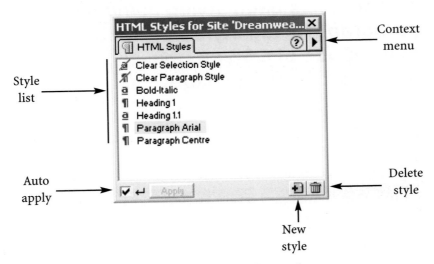

Figure 10.2 HTML Styles panel.

This text has been styled using the paragraph 'p' tag style.

```
 1 <html>
 2 <head>
 3 <title>HTML Tag style</title>
 4 <meta http-equiv="Content-Type" content="text/html; charset=iso-8859-1">
 5 <style type="text/css">
 6 <!--
 7 p {  font-family: Geneva, Arial, Helvetica, san-serif; font-size: 30px; font-weight: bold;
   color: #FF00FF;
 8 -->
 9 </style>
10 </head>
11 <body bgcolor="#FFFFFF" text="#000000">
12 <p>This text has been styled using the paragraph 'p' tag style.</p>
13 </body>
14 </html>
15
```

Figure 10.10 *Selecting a style via head content, in design view.*

This text has been styled using the paragraph 'p' tag style. We are also making use of CSS customized style to add a background image.

Figure 10.14 *Browser display for example in Figure 10.13.*

Figure 10.16 *Using CSS style to realize a rollover effect.*

invisible elements are provided in the preferences dialogue box. Choose Edit | Preferences and then the category Invisible Elements from the resulting dialogue box. We then have the option of choosing which element (marker) should be shown. This is depicted in Figure 6.33.

Figure 6.27 Selecting the Invisibles category on the Objects panel.

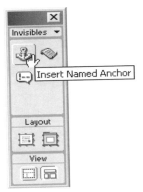

Figure 6.28 Using the Objects panel to insert a named anchor.

Figure 6.29 Inserting a named anchor on the fly.

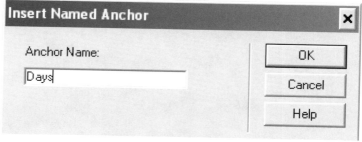

Figure 6.30 Insert Named Anchor dialogue box.

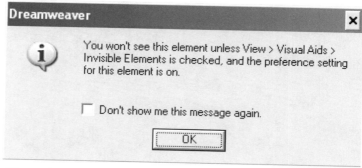

Figure 6.31 Warning message to say that anchor will be invisible.

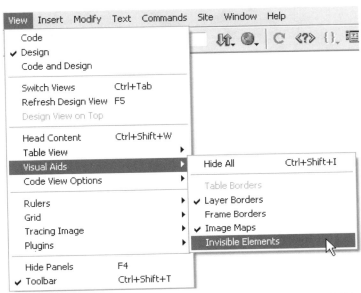

Figure 6.32 Option for making named anchor visible or invisible.

A corresponding marker for the named anchor is displayed at the insertion point on the page. This is shown in Figure 6.34, for the case depicted earlier in Figure 6.29. The name of the anchor can be edited, if required: open the Property Inspector panel and then select the anchor marker. This opens up the corresponding attributes for the named anchor. As Figure 6.35 shows, only the name parameter can be altered. Edit the existing name or type in a suitable new one in the text box. Note that the panel displays the anchor marker, as well as a label (NamedAnchor) to identify the panel contents.

Having created a named anchor, we are now in a position to produce a hyperlink. This will facilitate a viewer to jump to the position of the anchor marker. To build a link, do the following:

- Open the Property Inspector panel (Window | Properties).
- Choose Layout view from the Objects panel.

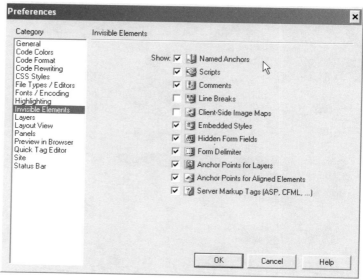

Figure 6.33 Invisible elements supported by Dreamweaver 4.0.

Named anchor marker

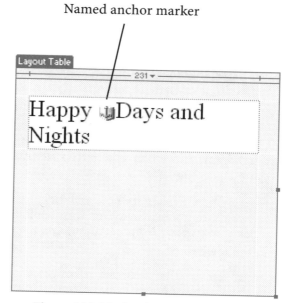

Figure 6.34 Marker for a named anchor.

Figure 6.35 Property Inspector panel for an anchor marker.

- Select some text (or an image) which will be the link to the named anchor.
- We can then create a link using the Property Inspector panel by any of the following three ways:
- Typing in the name of the named anchor in the Link box. This must be preceded by a hash (#), or
- Use the point-to-file icon (on the right of the Link box) to attach to an anchor marker. Figure 6.36 (also Plate XI) gives an illustration of this. As this portrays, the text 'Take me to the top!' is highlighted. We then use the point-to-file icon to create a link to the named anchor (topofpage). The environment automatically inserts the name of the anchor in the Link box; or
- From the selected text, press and hold down the Shift key and drag to the anchor marker. This is shown in Figure 6.37 (also Plate XII). The overall effect of doing this is the same as above whereby the environment automatically inserts the name of the anchor in the Link box.

Once a named anchor is created, it can be used by more than one hyperlink. In other words, we only need one named anchor at the top of a page, for example, and have several links pointing to it.

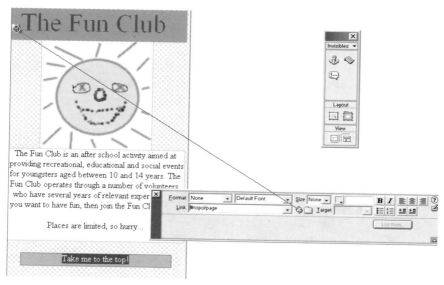

Figure 6.36 *Using point-to-file icon to create a hyperlink (also Plate XI).*

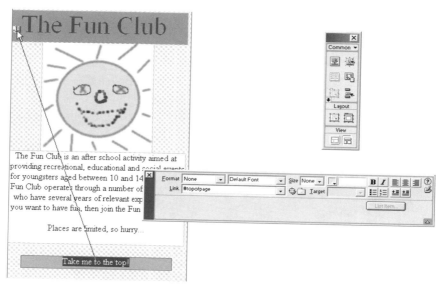

Figure 6.37 *Using Shift + drag to create a hyperlink (also Plate XII).*

Linking to other parts of a site

Being able to link within a page or to an external site through a URL is convenient. However, we also need to be able to move to other parts of the same site. A site typically has many pages (describing different aspects of a business, for example) and although each page may have been developed independently, hyperlinks are used to connect pages together.

The process of linking two or more pages together is similar to having a link within a page. We firstly create a named anchor and then create a hyperlink utilizing the created anchor. For example, on the first (home) page a menu is provided which points to information that resides on other pages. In this case, we would create named anchors on the other pages and then link these to the menu options appearing on the home page. Likewise, we would create a named anchor for the top of the home page and use this in the other pages to link back (that is, to return) to the home page.

The subtle difference between linking within and linking to another page is the fact that the named anchor in the latter case resides on a separate page. In order to use this, we must therefore give the address of the other page, together with the name of the anchor. That is, the location of the file containing the other page needs to be attached to the named anchor. This in practice resorts to specifying the filename, as the files belonging to a site are located in the same folder and we would be using relative addressing (for reasons described earlier in the chapter).

For example, if we had a named anchor (topofpage) within a file titled index.html, then for a selected text residing in another file, we would enter the following in the Link box: index.html#topofpage. This would create a hyperlink from the selected text to the named anchor.

As a site is developed, remembering (and therefore using) names of anchors can become tedious. A more convenient way for creating links would be to use the two visual forms discussed in the previous section. To achieve this, do the following:

- Open the first page (file) and place an anchor at the desired location.
- Next, open the second page (file) and highlight some text (or an image) which is to be used as a hyperlink.
- From the Property Inspector panel, click and drag the point-to-file icon associated with the Link parameter and release it on top of the named anchor marker. The corresponding hyperlink path is automatically entered in the Link text box. Figure 6.38 (also Plate XII) depicts the scenario: the words 'Take me home!' in file Named Anchor.htm are linked to the named anchor (topofpage) located in the file Page Link.htm.
- Alternatively, select the text and use Shift and drag to the named anchor marker. The link address automatically appears in the Link box, highlighting the fact that a hyperlink between the two pages has been generated.

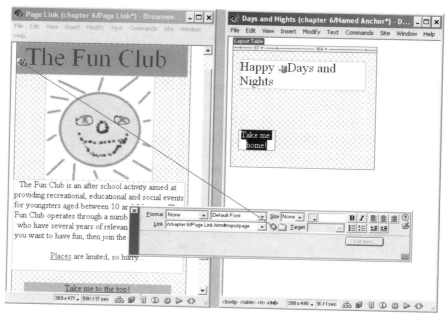

Figure 6.38 *Creating a hyperlink between two pages (files) (also Plate XII).*

Adding a Mailto link

Most professional web sites, and even those less professional, have a way of allowing viewers to contact them by electronic mail (email). In order for this to be realized, a link needs to be established on a page, which when selected by the viewer opens a default email application (such as Microsoft Outlook). The link is referred to as a Mailto link. We make use of the Objects panel to insert the link. As Figure 6.39 depicts, within the Common category of the panel, we choose the Insert Email Link icon.

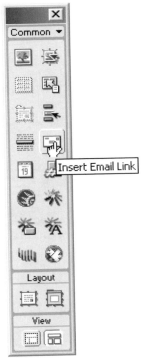

Figure 6.39 Using the Objects panel to add a mail link.

The result of choosing the respective icon is a dialogue box, which requires two parameters: the first being the text that will be used as the link to invoke the mail application programme. The second parameter is the email address where a message is to be sent. Figure 6.40 shows an illustrative example.

An alternative to the above approach is to select a text from a page and then to click on the Insert Email Link icon on the Objects panel. As Figure 6.41 shows, this will open up the corresponding dialogue box with the selected text within the Text box. The Dreamweaver 4.0 environment automatically inserts the email address that was previously used. Edit contents of either text boxes as desired.

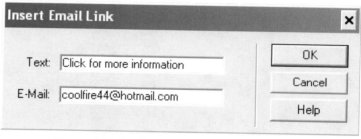

Figure 6.40 *Setting-up an email link on a page.*

Figure 6.41 *Selecting text for emailing purposes.*

Chapter 7

Working with Layers

Introduction

We have seen how cells and tables can be used to realize a design layout. These act as placeholders for text blocks, images, hyperlinks and other elements. An extension of this concept and more in tune with the dynamic nature of a web site is to employ layers. These give added control and flexibility in positioning and managing HTML elements. Moreover, the use of layers facilitates animation on a page, through the application of timelines. A page can have a number of layers, each one containing a separate element. This way, for example, a company logo could be embedded on the bottom layer and the contents of the site on the top layers. Images on a page could be shown to go through a transitional effect, where they fade in and out of the page. Although, these and other effects can be realized using JavaScript (together with HTML codes), the Dreamweaver 4.0 environment provides a visual way of undertaking these without the direct need of program codes.

The potential and implementation of layers for creating a web page should be done with the understanding that not all web browsers will be able to display them. Internet Explorer 4.0 and Netscape 4.0 and later versions support layers. Tables therefore provide a more convenient way of expressing a page layout (since they have broader browser support) and, as such, the Dreamweaver 4.0 environment has features which allow for the conversion of layers to tables and vice versa.

This chapter begins by showing how to insert layers on a page and what parameters (that is, attributes) are associated with layers and how these can be adjusted to gain a desired page layout. The discussion then focuses on using layers and timelines to develop animations.

Establishing layer preferences

Before adding a layer to a page, it is worth looking at the default values for the layer parameters. These are located on the preferences dialogue box. Choose `Edit | Preferences` to open the dialogue box. Then choose Layers as the category. As Figure 7.1 depicts, here we can establish the default tag, visibility, width, height, background colour, background image, and whether nesting (more on this later on this chapter) is permissible. The Netscape 4 Compatibility option allows the Dreamweaver 4.0 environment to automatically insert the Netscape Layer Fix. The problem this addresses is the resizing of layers (and therefore the contents of a page) when the Netscape browser window is enlarged or made small.

The insertion of the fix can be done automatically (via the mentioned preference option) or it can be manually established through using the main menu. In the latter case, choose `Command | Add/Remove Netscape Resize Fix`. The scenario is illustrated in Figure 7.2. When the option is

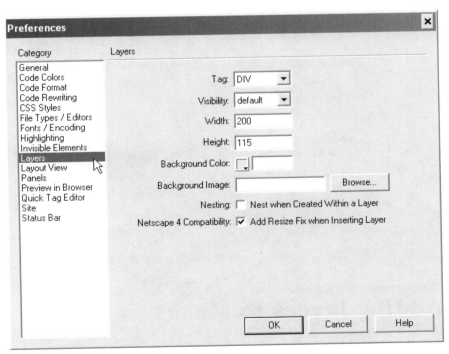

Figure 7.1 Layer settings within the Preference dialogue box.

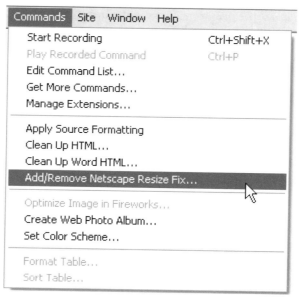

Figure 7.2 Option to manually insert Netscape Resize Fix.

selected, the message box shown in Figure 7.3 automatically appears to say why the fix is necessary. The Dreamweaver 4.0 environment includes a JavaScript function within the document to help repair the shortcoming. The manual option works on a page and needs to be inserted again on each new page that is developed.

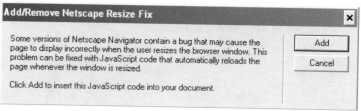

Figure 7.3 Message box providing need for Netscape Resize Fix.

Adding layers to a page

We can insert a layer on a page by either making use of the main menu or the Objects panel. To do this, first select standard (page) view by choosing View | Table View and then Standard View, or through clicking the respective icon on the Objects panel. Then choose any of the three options listed below:

- Select Insert | Layer to add a new layer at the insertion point on the page. The attributes associated with the layer will be those set as default in the preferences dialogue box; or
- Click the Draw Layer icon on the Objects panel. Figure 7.4 shows the location of the icon. We are now in a position to draw a layer at a desired location on a page: use the crosshair to position and then click and drag out a layer of required size. Figure 7.5 shows an animated illustration creating a layer using this approach; or

Figure 7.4 Draw Layer icon on the Objects panel.

Essential Dreamweaver 4.0 *fast*

● Position the insertion point at a desired location on the page. Then click the Draw Layer icon on the Objects panel and drag it onto the page. When the icon (cursor) is released over the page, a layer is automatically added at the location of the insertion point (irrespective of where the icon is released). The attributes (for example, size) are those set as default within the preferences dialogue box. Figure 7.6 depicts the scenario.

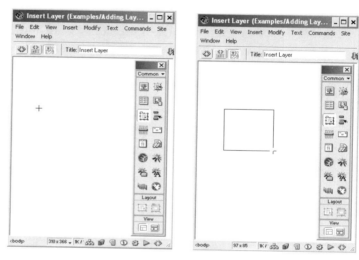

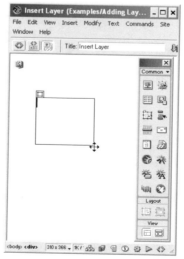

Figure 7.5 Creation of a layer using click and drag approach.

If we wanted to create more than one layer at a time, we will need to make use of the control (CTRL) key. The way this works is to hold down the CTRL key and then use the second option described above to draw a layer. Additional layers can then be drawn through the same approach whilst the CTRL key is held down.

As Figure 7.7 shows when a layer is drawn, two components appear on the page: one being the layer and the other a layer marker. The latter are part of what the Dreamweaver 4.0 environment refers to as the Invisible Elements. We can toggle their display on or off by choosing View | Visual Aids and then Invisible Elements. As mentioned in the previous chapter, we can use the preferences dialogue box to set default display options for all invisible elements supported by the environment.

Although the Layer marker (like the rest of the invisible elements) are displayed when designing a page, they are taken as hidden elements as far as browsers are concerned. In other words, they are not displayed in a browser window. When the elements are toggled on to be visible on a design page, other components are appropriately shifted. The non-display of these within a browser means that any shifting that

Figure 7.6 Creation of a layer click and drop approach.

may have taken place within the document window is ignored and the components of a page are positioned without any adjustments.

As we will discuss later on in this chapter, layers can be created within existing layers and we can establish settings to ensure that when two layers are created, they do not overlap.

Layer
Marker

Layer

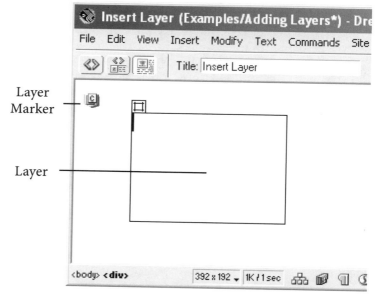

Figure 7.7 Addition of a layer on a page.

Positioning layers

Once we have placed a layer (or layers) on a page, we can change their position by firstly selecting it and then dragging it to a new location. The selection of a layer can be made through any of the following ways:

- By clicking the layer marker; or
- Through clicking on the layer's selection handle. This, as Figure 7.8 depicts, is located on the top left of the layer. If this handle is not visible then place the cursor within the layer and click once; or

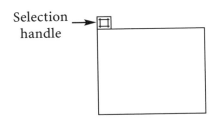

Selection handle

Figure 7.8 Selection handle on a layer.

- Clicking on the outline (that is, border) of the layer; or
- If no selection handle is visible, then using the Shift key and clicking inside a layer; or
- Through choosing the desired layer in the layer panel. The panel can be opened using the function key F2 or via `Window | Layers`. More discussion on the layer panel later on in this chapter.

Once a layer is selected, it is highlighted with eight resizing handles. This is shown in Figure 7.9. Selection of two or more layers, residing on a page, can also be made. This time, we will need to use the Shift and click combination to either choose the layers from the layer panel, or to select through clicking on the borders of the respective layers. As Figure 7.10 shows, when two or more layers are selected, the last layer to be selected has black resizing handles, whilst the others have white coloured handles.

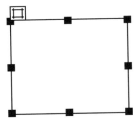

Figure 7.9 A selected layer has eight resizing handles.

We can move a layer by a number of different ways. For a selected layer, we can use any one of the three approaches outlined below:

- Click the selection handle of a layer and drag it to a new location. Figure 7.11 provides an animated illustration of how this operates.
- Click on the border of a layer (not any of the resizing handles) and drag the layer to a desired position.
- Use the arrow keys to move the layer one pixel in a particular direction. Combining this with the Shift key provides greater (usually ten pixel) increments. Use View | Grid and then Snap to Grid to move to fixed points on a page.

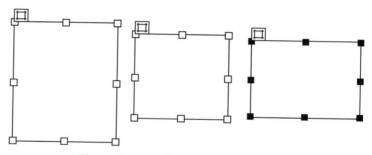

Figure 7.10   Multiple selection of layers.

Resizing layers

We can resize a single layer or a group of selected layers (to synchronize width and height dimensions, for example) through a number of ways. To resize a selected layer, do one of the following:

- Use any of the eight available handles on the layer border to resize as required; or
- Hold down the control (CTRL) key and use the arrow keys to resize in the desired direction. This will increment the layer by one pixel at a time; or
- Combine the CTRL key with the Shift key to scale by greater increments (usually 10 pixels) by using the arrows to specify direction of resize; or
- Use the Property Inspector panel (see next section below).

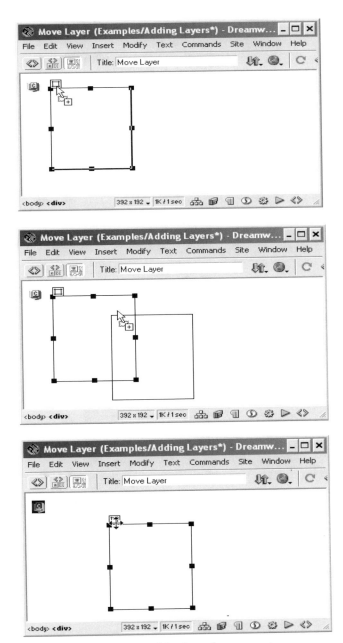

Figure 7.11 *Repositioning a layer on a page.*

Resizing a layer does not affect the contents of a layer. In other words, the properties (such as the size of an image) remain unchanged unless defined otherwise. It also does not define the visible area, as this is controlled via other parameters available on the Property Inspector panel.

Two or more selected layers can be scaled at the same time to match their width and height values. We use Modify |

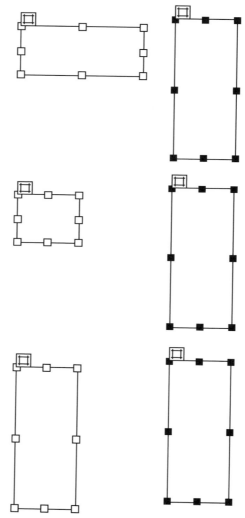

Figure 7.12 Resizing two layers to match width and height.

Align and then Make Same Width or Make Same Height to respectively adjust the dimensions. The resulting dimensions are referenced on the last selected layer. In other words, the layer whose handles are shown as black is used as the basis for setting the width and height of any other selected layer. Figure 7.12 provides an animated illustration of this scenario for two selected layers: the top part shows original sizes, the middle part the effect of matching widths, whilst the bottom part shows heights of the two layers being normalized.

We can alternatively use the Property Inspector panel to resize multiple selected layers. This, together with other properties of layers, is discussed in the next section.

Understanding layer properties

Attributes associated with a selected layer (or layers) are presented within the Property Inspector panel. The panel can be opened by a variety of means, including the following:

● Select Modify | Selection Properties; or
● Choose Window | Properties; or
● Right click on the respective layer marker whilst the layer is not selected. The effect of this is to both select the layer and open a context menu. Figure 7.13 shows the resulting context menu for a layer. From this, choose Properties to open the Property Inspector panel. The context menu can also be opened using the layer selection handle (located top left on the layer) when the layer has already been selected. Note that there is a context menu associated with the layer. This appears when the cursor is within the layer and a right click is made. The menu does not contain an option to open the panel.

The Property Inspector panel for a selected layer is depicted in Figure 7.14. As this shows there are a number of attributes associated with a layer. Let us start with the two that were presented in the previous two sections; namely, reposition and resize.

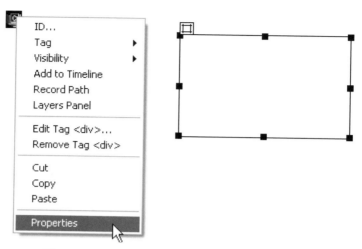

Figure 7.13 Using context menu to open Property
Inspector panel for the selected layer.

To change the position of a layer, we make use of the L and T parameters. These respectively stand for the left and top coordinates of a layer, in pixels. The position of the layer is with reference to the origin (0,0), located at the top left corner of a page (or of a parent layer if nested – more on nested layers later on this chapter). In other words, if L was set to 40 pixels and T to 70 pixels, then the layer would be positioned 40 pixels from the left edge of the page and 70 pixels from the top of the page. The scenario is portrayed in Figure 7.15. We can use other units apart from pixels by appending the appropriate abbreviations next to the coordinate value(s) without leaving a space. For example, an entry of 20 inches will be written as 20in.

The W and H parameters respectively refer to the width and height of the selected layer. We can use these to specify (and

Figure 7.14 Property Inspector panel for a layer.

hence change) the dimensions of a layer. If the contents of the layer expand beyond the specified size then entries in W and H are normally overwritten.

Each layer has a unique identity, which is realized through the Layer ID parameter. This allows a layer to be named. The name appears in the Layers panel and thus enables for quick selection of the layer. In addition, the name can be used to reference the Layer and its attributes when scripting is incorporated for page design.

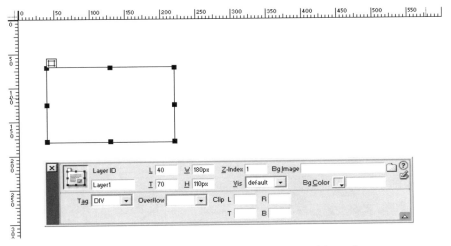

Figure 7.15 *Use of L and T parameters to position a layer.*

To enter a name, we make use of the text box associated with the Layer ID parameter on the Property Inspector panel. Figure 7.16 shows an example. Alternatively, we can make use of the context menu linked with the layer marker and the layer selection handle. Right click opens the context menu and, as Figure 7.17 depicts, we choose ID from the list of options. This in turn opens the text box shown in Figure 7.18. Enter a name for the layer and press OK. The Layer ID parameter on the Property Inspector panel gets automatically updated with the new name entered via the context menu.

Figure 7.16 *Using Layer ID text box to label a layer.*

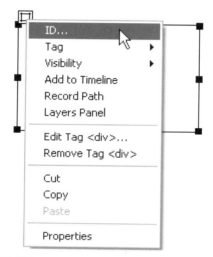

Figure 7.17 *Using context menu to open layer ID box.*

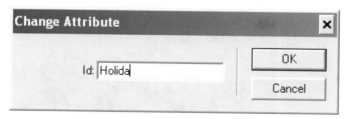

Figure 7.18 *Layer ID box.*

When entering a name for a layer, ensure that no spaces, periods, hyphens, etc, are included, as the environment will respond with an error message. Although numbers can be used, a layer name cannot begin with a number. Therefore, valid names are Boat22, Car45, FH786, and the like; whilst 1Ace, Shoe-Show, Tree.57, etc, will not be accepted.

We can choose the Bg Image parameter (on the Property Inspector panel) to insert a background image in a layer. Either type the path to an image file in the text box or use the folder icon to browse for a suitable image. Figure 7.19 (also Plate XIII) shows an example, where we note that an image smaller than the layer will be tiled (appearing enough times to fill the layer).

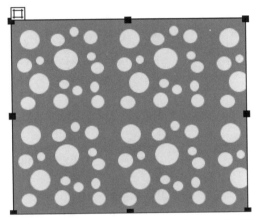

Figure 7.19 Adding a background image to a layer (also Plate XIII).

The Bg Color parameter can be used to have a background colour, instead of an image. In this case, simply select a desired colour using the pull-down menu (palette) or enter a corresponding colour number in the text box associated with the parameter. We can choose to either have a background image or a background colour. The image normally takes precedence if both are applied. As mentioned earlier in this chapter, default background image and colour is set through the preferences dialogue box.

Defining layer visible region

Sometimes it is necessary to use the layer as a placeholder for, say, an image. However, we may want to make only a portion of the image visible. To do this, we use the Clip parameter on the Property Inspector panel. Figure 7.20 shows its location on the panel. As we can see from this, four values can be used for clipping. These define the visible area for the layer. L and R respectively refer to the left and right, whilst T and B denote top and bottom. It is important to realize that these values are distances from the respective layer edges and not the page margins.

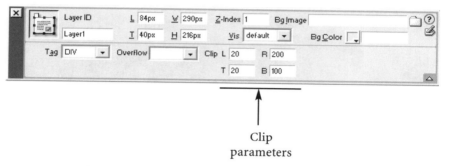

Clip
parameters

Figure 7.20 Settings for defining visible layer regions.

The way the clipping feature works is that the difference between R and L, and B and T, define the visible region. Both R and L refer to the left edge of the layer. B and T use the top edge. The best way to understand this is through an example: we want to clip the image shown in Figure 7.21 (also Plate XIII) so that the height is 80 pixels and the width 180 pixels. The visible region of interest is 20 pixels from the left edge and 20 pixels from the top. In other words, the top left corner of the visible region is located at (20, 20). This results in the following settings for the four clip parameters:

- L = 20
- R = 20+180 = 200
- T = 20
- B = 20+80 = 100

The result of clipping using these values is shown in Figure 7.22. If, at any stage, we wanted to quickly view the hidden parts of an image, place the cursor on the border or inside a layer and click once. Alternatively, double click and the file

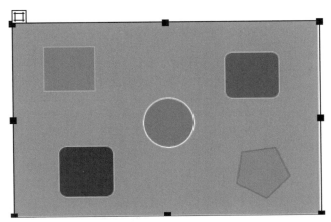

Figure 7.21 *Layer containing an image to be clipped (also Plate XIII).*

folder containing the image will open. This contains a preview, together with original size of the image. We can also see the full image on the thumbnail that appears on the Property Inspector panel when the image is selected. In fact, the thumbnail can be used to show the complete image within the layer: click once on the thumbnail to see the complete image. To see only the visible region, select the layer or click once within the layer.

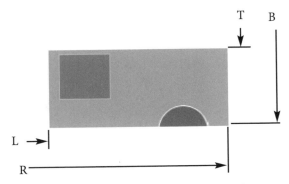

Figure 7.22 *Layer containing a clipped image.*

Having defined a clip area, if we then change the source of an image (in other words, chose another image to replace an existing one in the layer) then the visible region is still applicable. This means that the new image will continue to be visible within the defined region. We can change the source file either through the Property Inspector panel when the image is selected (using the Src parameter, as discussed in the previous chapter) or through using the context menu associated with the layer. Figure 7.23 shows the available option (Source File) on the context menu.

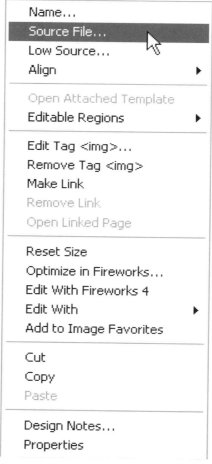

Figure 7.23 Context menu for a layer.

Working with multiple layers

A number of distinctive features exist when working with two or more selected layers. We can, for example, set background colour of several layers with one stroke. Likewise, the size and position can also be adjusted and synchronized. In addition, two or more layers can be aligned through a number of options. We can also have nested layers. That is a layer (or layers) added to a base layer. In this section, we will look at how to work with these (and other) attributes related to multiple layers.

The Property Inspector panel for selected multiple layers is different than for a single layer. Figure 7.24 shows the contents of the panel when two or more layers are selected.

Figure 7.24 Property Inspector panel for multiple selected layers.

The Property Inspector panel is effectively split into two halves: top and bottom. The top represents attributes related to text, whilst the bottom (headed Multiple Layers) covers the layer parameters. The two parameters L and T are used to position the selected layers, whilst W and H facilitate resizing. The way these work is as follows:

- L stands for left and determines the distance (in pixels) from the left edge of a page (or parent layer if nested).
- T stands for top and specifies the distance from the top edge of a page (or parent layer if nested). Figure 7.25 shows an example of two layers. The top image shows the original positions, whilst the bottom image depicts the scenario for repositioning of 40 pixels from the left edge and 60 pixels from the top edge. In other words, the layer's top left corner is located at (40, 60).

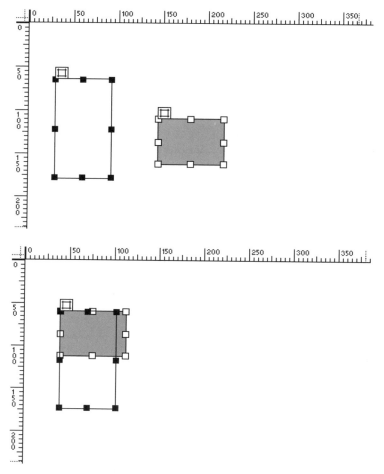

Figure 7.25 Repositioning multiple layers.

- W stands for width and sets the width of the selected layers if contents are within new values.
- H stands for height and sets the height of selected layers if contents are within new values. Figure 7.26 manifests the case where the width and height of the two selected layers has been changed respectively to 200 and 100 pixels.

As Figure 7.26 depicts, the contents of one of the two layers is visible since the size and position of both layers has been

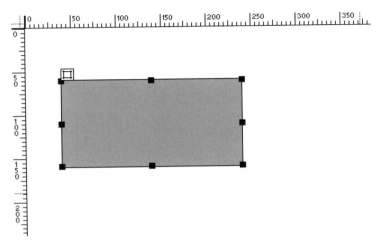

Figure 7.26 *Effect of resizing (width and height) of multiple layers.*

made the same. To view the contents of the bottom layer, select layers and then do one of the following:

- Choose Modify | Arrange and then Send to Back.
- Use the Z-index parameter on the Property Inspector panel. Figure 7.27 depicts the location of this on the panel. The Z dimension returns the depth (of a page), whilst the z-index provides the stacking order of layers. In order words, the number entered in the text box associated with the z-index establishes the position of a layer in a pack. Higher numbered layers are closer to the front and, therefore, appear above lower numbered layers.
- Alternatively, we can use the Layers panel to view a desired layer, or to change the z-index. Choose Window | Layers to open the panel. Figure 7.28 shows an example of the resulting panel. To view the contents of a desired layer, simply click on the layer name.

The Layers can also be used to change the stacking order. There are two ways of doing this: the first approach makes use of the Z column. Here, we select a cell corresponding to a layer whose z-index we wish to change. Type a number to reflect movement of the layer in relation to the stack. As mentioned above, a higher number will bring the layer to the

Stacking order
parameter

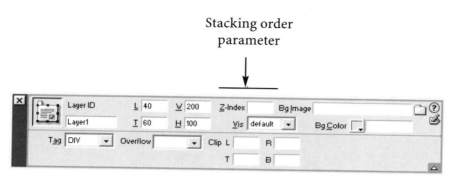

Figure 7.27 Z-index parameter on the Property Inspector panel.

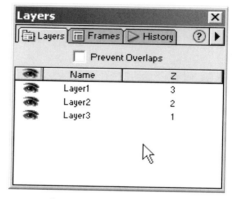

Figure 7.28 Layers panel.

top of the stack and, therefore, the display of its contents will take precedence over lower numbered layers. Figure 7.29 gives an animated illustration, highlighting the fact that once a number is entered, the stack is automatically sorted to reflect this change.

The second method that can be used to reorder a stack makes use of click and drag: within the Layers panel, use the Name column to select a desired layer. We then move the layer up (or down) to adjust its position with the stack. As animated in Figure 7.30, when a layer is selected and dragged, a line appears to indicate position. Using this as a reference point, release the mouse key to move the layer to this level within

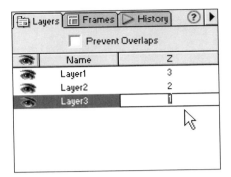
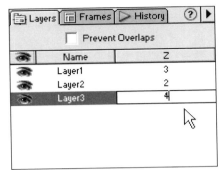
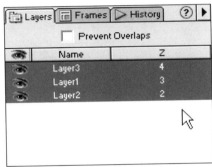

Figure 7.29 Changing layer stack order via the Z column.

the stack. The Dreamweaver 4.0 environment automatically updates the Z column to highlight the reordering of layers.

We can also change the background colour of selected layers. The process for doing this is similar to that for a single layer. Choose Bg Color parameter on the Property Inspector panel. Likewise, a background image can be added to multiple selected layers by attaching an image file to the Bg Image parameter.

Two or more layers can be aligned through using the main menu. The alignment is with reference to the border of the last layer that was selected (shown with black handles). Alignment can also affect nested layers, if the parent layer is involved in the process. More on nested layers in the next section.

To align selected layers, choose Modify | Align and then the four possible alignments options: left, right, top, or

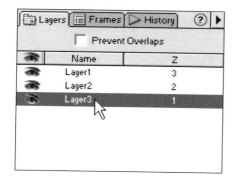 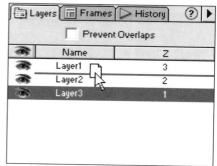

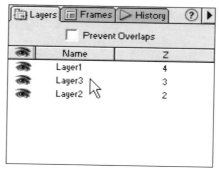

Figure 7.30 Changing layer stack order via the Name column.

bottom. The workings of each are illustrated in Figure 7.31, where alignment is applied in the sequence shown, starting from the top.

Understanding nested layers

Layers can be added to an existing layer (or layers). When this happens, new layers are nested within the existing layer and the set-up is generally referred to as nested layers. The term parent and child layer points to the fact that an existing layer (parent) has certain attributes that are shared with the embedded layers (children). This includes, for example, the visibility properties of a parent layer. Figure 7.32 gives an illustration of nested layers.

To produce nested layers, start by creating a parent layer and then do one of the following:

- Place the insertion point inside the parent layer and choose Insert | Layer. This will add a (child) layer of dimensions specified in the parent references dialogue box; or
- Click the Draw Layer button on the Objects panel and drag it onto the parent layer. The insertion point automatically appears within the parent layer to indicate that the object (in this case, a layer) can be added. Drop the selection inside the parent layer to add a layer of default settings; or
- Press and hold down the Alt key and then click on the Draw Layer button on the Objects panel. Position the crosshair at a specified location within the parent layer and draw a layer of a desired dimensions; or
- Check the nesting option on the preferences dialogue box (Edit | Preferences, and then the Layers category). All layers that are created within an parent layer are nested; irrespective of the way they are created.

The Layers panel provides a visual way of looking at nested layers, as well as a means for adjusting layer relationships. Figure 7.33 depicts an example: Layer2 and Layer3 are children of the parent layer, Layer1; whilst Layer4 is a single layer on a page.

We can use the Layers panel to either include a layer into an existing nest or to create an entirely new nest. Let us look at the example shown in Figure 7.34: Layer1 contains child layers (Layer2 and Layer3), whilst Layer4 contains a child layer (Layer5). Layer5 is the parent for Layer6. In essence, Layer6 is the grandchild of Layer4. The figure illustrates the case where we want to make Layer4 part of Layer1. In other words, Layer4 and its siblings (Layer5 and Layer6) to become a nest of the parent layer, Layer1.

With reference to Figure 7.34, we can nest a layer within another layer by making use of drag and drop. Press and hold down the CTRL (control) key and then select the desired layer which is going become the child of another. As we move up and down the Name column, layers are highlighted by a box outline. This identifies potential parent layers. Choose the desired parent layer by releasing the mouse button.

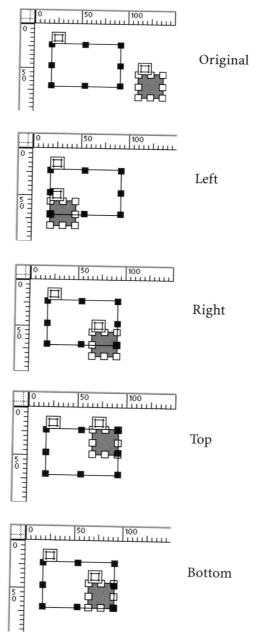

Figure 7.31 Aligning layers via Modify | Align.

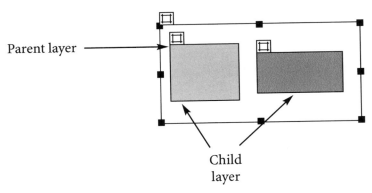

Parent layer

Child
layer

Figure 7.32 *Nested layers.*

The Layers panel can also assist us in other ways. For example, we may want to view only some layers and hide others. Moreover, we may want a child layer to follow a parent layers visibility settings. The column headed with an eye icon can assist us here since its purpose is to control the visibility of layers. There are three possible visibility states for a layer. These are shown in Table 7.1, where the inheritance option from the page results in the child layers being visible. This is because the page contents are always visible.

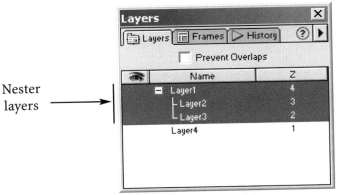

Nester
layers

Figure 7.33 *Layers panel showing nested layers.*

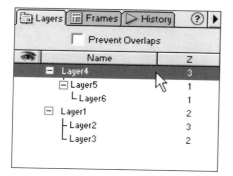
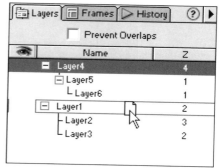
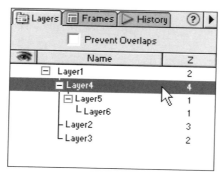

Figure 7.34 *Creating nested layers via the Layers panel.*

Table 7.1 Visibility options for a layer within the Layers panel.

Eye Icon	Visibility State
👁	Make layer visible.
👁	Make layer invisible.
(no icon)	Inherit visibility state from parent (or page if not nested).

To apply the visibility states to a layer, we place the mouse pointer over the respective cell within the eye icon column. Figure 7.35 depicts the scenario. A single click changes the state. If a layer is visible then on each click the states will change to inheritance, invisible, visible, and so on.

The inheritance state highlights a potential difficulty when layers are taken out of a nest. The problem is related to the fact that the parent of the layer has changed. Since some attributes

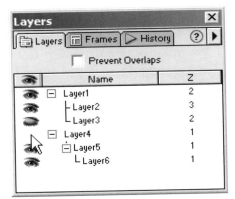

Figure 7.35 *Changing the layer visibility state via eye icon column.*

of a layer are linked to its parent, we should expect to manually adjust for this. For example, the position of a child layer is linked to its parent layer. Changing the parent layer will result in a change of position for the child layer. We can make use of the Property Inspector panel to edit attributes related to the (child) layer, including position. Simply select the layer from the Layers panel and then open the Property Inspector panel for fine-tuning the child layer attributes.

Using layer and table relationships

As mentioned earlier, there is a need to translate layers (and their respective) content to tables and cells. This is so that most browsers will be able to successfully render (display) a web site. There is also a need, sometimes, to convert tables and cells into layers. The Dreamweaver 4.0 environment supports both options.

For conversion options, we make use of the main menu. Choose Modify | Convert and then either Tables to Layers, or Layers to Table. Figure 7.36 depicts the scenario. Before converting layers to table, ensure that layers do not overlap, since overlap feature cannot be entertained within a table. The Layers panel can be used to control the overlap attribute.

Open the panel and check the box labelled Prevent Overlaps. Figure 7.37 gives an illustration.

When the option to convert from layers to table is chosen, a corresponding dialogue box is activated. As Figure 7.38 shows, the dialogue box has a number of parameters that can be used to customize the conversion. These include:

- Most Accurate. This is the recommended option since it converts every layer to a cell and adds extra cells to cover spaces on a page.
- Smallest. Layers are converted into cells, but empty spaces within a defined threshold are ignored. The page layout, therefore, is likely to change when converted. Figure 7.39 gives an example of using both options: the top image is the original, which uses two layers. The bottom left image is the conversion table using the Most Accurate option, whilst the bottom right image uses Smallest option (with threshold set at 10 pixels).

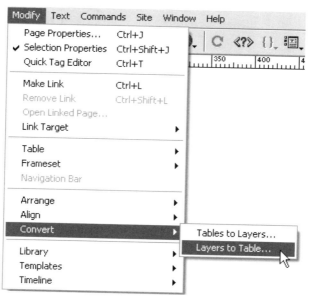

Figure 7.36 *Options for conversion between layers and tables.*

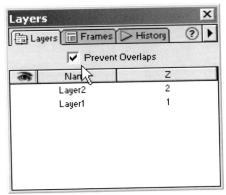

Figure 7.37 *Checkbox for controlling layer overlaps.*

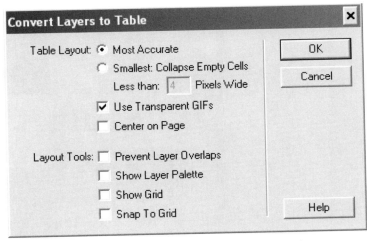

Figure 7.38 *Convert layers to table dialogue box.*

- Use Transparent GIFs. The purpose of this parameter is to prevent empty table columns from contracting and thus affecting the page layout. By checking this option, the environment adds transparent GIFs in the last row of the table.
- Center on Page. Tables are by default left aligned. By checking this option, the table will be aligned to the centre of the page.

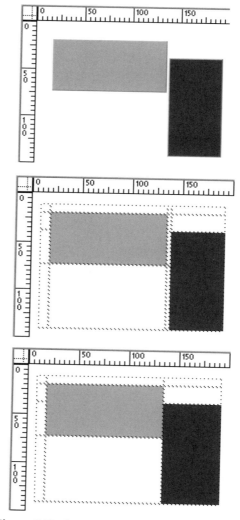

Figure 7.39 *Conversion of layers to tables.*

- Click OK, after choosing (if any) of the tool and grid options.

The dialogue box for converting from tables to layers is shown in Figure 7.40. Effectively, each cell that has content will be converted into a layer. Empty cells will be used to insert (white) space to preserve page layout.

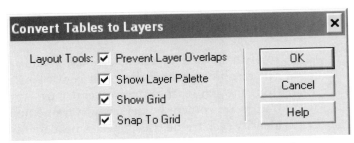

Figure 7.40 Convert tables to layers dialogue box.

Understanding animation

Animation provides a powerful way of expressing a message and gaining attention, especially when employed for web delivery. The Dreamweaver 4.0 environment has a range of tools to assist us in developing animation quickly. The approach used is similar to other Macromedia products, such as Director and Flash.

Animation makes use of frames. Frames in turn contain the content. Having several frames appear and then disappear, with different content, over a span of time, results in an animation. If, for example, we had a layer whose contents remained the same, but its position on the page was changing over time, we would gain motion. Having motion allows us to create animation. Alternatively, we could use the z-index to change the ordering of layers over time. This will have the effect of contents appearing and disappearing over a span of time and as such is animation.

Using the timelines panel

The key point to realize from the previous section is that to create animation, we need a timeline. The timeline needs to have contents that are changing. Change can take several forms including position, visibility and size. The

Dreamweaver 4.0 environment has a timeline panel which forms the basis for generating animated features on a page.

To open the timelines panel, choose `Window | Timelines`. The resulting panel is shown in Figure 7.41. As can be seen from the figure, there are several parts to the panel: the frames are content holders, whilst frame number is used to identify each frame. The playback head identifies the current frame and can be moved to a desired frame by clicking and dragging. The channels allow multiple objects to be animated at the same time. For example, we could have two birds flying in opposite directions. We may decide to use a channel for the first bird and a different channel for the second. This would provide better control over events.

Once an animation is created, we can use the playback controls to view contents of each frame. These are located at the top of the timelines panel. Figure 7.42 shows the set of buttons and options that are available. These can be summarized as follows:

- Rewind. Moves the playback head to the first frame in the animation.
- Back. Moves the playback head one frame to the left. By holding down the button, the animation plays in reverse.
- Current frame. Location of playback head. Enter a (frame) number in the text box to reposition the playback head.
- Play. Moves the playback head one frame to the right. By holding down the button, the animation plays in normal mode.
- Fps = Frames per second. This, as the name suggests, determines the number of frames to be played in every second. Enter a high number in the text box if an animation needs to run at a pace, or to smooth out an animation that runs across a page. Typically, for web usage a fps of 15 to 25 is sufficient. In some cases, the browser will not respond to an even higher setting. A low fps may result in flicker being apparent. This is the transition going from one frame to the next. If the rate is fast enough then the eye is not able to pick this up.

Otherwise, the animation will look jerky. Much will depend on the nature of the animation and particularly on the contents of the frames when deciding fps.

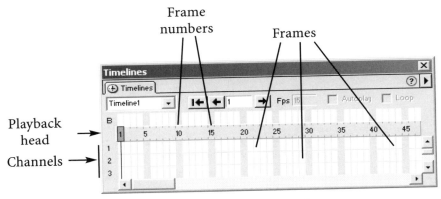

Figure 7.41 The Timelines panel.

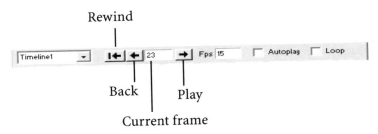

Figure 7.42 Playback controls on the timelines panel.

Creating a simple animation

There are a variety of ways to create an animation within the Dreamweaver 4.0 environment. All of the approaches make use of layers. The simplest approach uses a line to define a path for the animation. The steps necessary for generating such an animation are as follows:

● Move the playback head (on the timelines panel) to frame 1. This sets the start frame of the animation. It is not necessary to set the playback head to frame 1, but for our purposes here we will use the first frame.

- Select and position the layer to be animated. This effectively establishes the contents of the first frame.
- Next, choose `Modify | Timeline` and then Record Path of Layer. This is shown in Figure 7.43.
- We are now ready to define a path for the animation. By moving the layer to a new location on the page, a line is drawn which represents the path. As Figure 7.44 (also Plate XIV) depicts, the path does not necessary need to be a straight line. It can be curved. The top image in Figure 7.44 (also Plate XIV) shows the case where the layer is moving and a path is drawn as a thick line. When the layer reaches its destination (new position and end of animation), the path is shown as normal line. The bottom

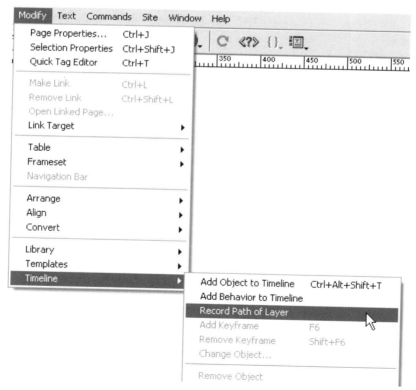

Figure 7.43 Option to define an animation path.

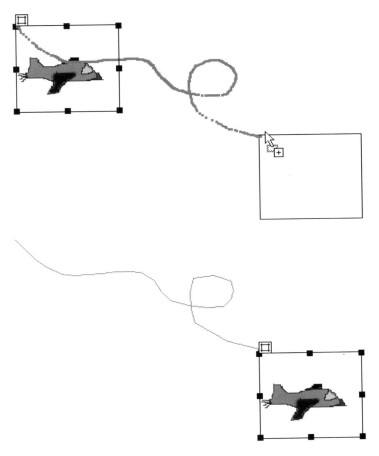

Figure 7.44 Defining an animation path (also Plate XIV).

       image in Figure 7.44 (also Plate XIV) illustrates this state.
Note that the top left corner of the layer lies on the path.

- Once a path is defined, the Dreamweaver 4.0 environment generates an animation bar in the timelines panel. This is shown in Figure 7.45 (also Plate XIV) (for the animation manifested in Figure 7.44).

Having developed an animation, we would naturally want to see it running. This is achieved by moving the playback head across the span of the animation. We can manually click and drag the head to move through the frames. Alternatively, the Play button (on the timelines panel) can be held down for the same effect. The Back button can also be used if we want to view the animation in reverse.

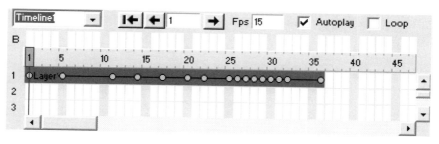

Figure 7.45 *Animation bar on the timelines panel (also Plate XIV).*

In addition, the Autoplay and Loop options on the timelines panel (see Figure 7.45 (also Plate XIV)) can be used to view the animation within a browser. Choose Autoplay to upload the animation as the browser opens. This will run the animation once. If we needed to repeat the animation then we would also check the Loop option.

We can name a timeline by using the pull-down (menu) text box located on the timelines panel. As Figure 7.46 depicts, the name "Plane" has been added for the animation created in this section. Giving timelines names provides a useful way of referencing them.

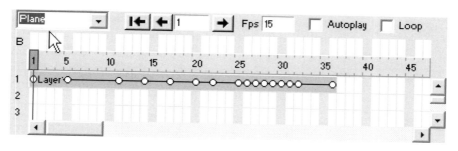

Figure 7.46 *Naming a timeline.*

Creating animation via keyframes

An alternative method for producing an animation is by inserting a layer to the timeline and using the resulting keyframes to manually fine-tune an animation. We have actually encountered keyframes already in the previous section. Along an animation bar (such as shown in Figure 7.46), keyframes are shown as solid circles. Keyframes differ from normal frames in that they reflect change and can, therefore, be used to edit change.

To add an animation using this approach, we need to follow the steps listed below. We will assume that the new animation will be located in the second channel on the timelines panel. The steps are as follows:

- Select the layer (not its contents).
- Next, either choose `Modify | Timeline` and then Add Object to Timeline, or drag and drop the layer on the first frame of the second channel. This results in the scenario shown in Figure 7.47, where an animation bar appears. We can reposition the bar by dragging and dropping it at a desired location within a channel.
- To produce an animation, click on the end keyframe (for Layer2, frame 15 in Figure 7.47) and then move the layer on the page to a new (where the animation should stop) location. The result of doing this is that a straight path is

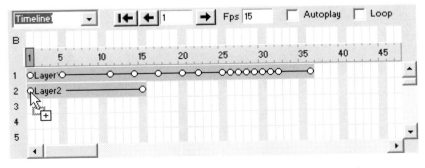

Figure 7.47 Adding a layer (Layer2) to timelines panel.

drawn on the page. This is shown in Figure 7.48, where Layer2 is shown containing a ball image.

- Likewise, if we needed to reposition the beginning of the animation, click on the start keyframe and manually adjust location of the layer on the page.
- To view the animation, use either Play or Back button, or select Autoplay and then press function key F12 to run the animation in a browser.

A curved path can be derived through inserting additional keyframes along the path. Keyframes can be inserted to a selected timeline either by choosing Modify | Timelines and then Add Keyframe option, or by pressing function key F6, or using the context menu associated with the selected layer. In all cases, a new keyframe will be inserted at the location of the playback head. Alternatively, we can use the control (CTRL) key to interactively insert keyframes. In this case, as we hover over a timeline (with CTRL pressed down), the cursor changes shape to that of a keyframe (a solid circle). When this happens, click on a frame to convert to a keyframe.

Figure 7.49 illustrates an example of how we can use an inserted keyframe to define a curved path. In this case, the

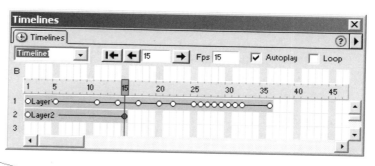

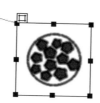

Figure 7.48 Creating an animation path through the end keyframe.

layer is repositioned at the new keyframe, causing the path to change from a straight line to a curved outline.

If we needed to make use of an existing timeline for a newly created layer then we apply the Change Object option to swap layers for a timeline. The option is available via the context menu, or through `Modify | Timeline`.

In addition to changing the layer position, other attributes of a layer (or layers) can also vary through a timeline. The most common would be to create a transition effect through fading in and out contents of layers. This can be done either by phasing visibility or changing the z-index of layers.

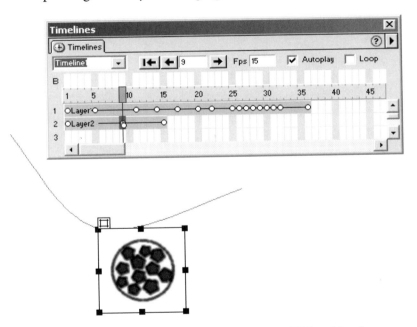

Figure 7.49 Changing animation path via an additional keyframe.

Chapter

8

Working with Frames

Introduction

For a number of reasons, web designs and web sites make use of frames. For the most part this is to assist the usability aspects of a site. We may have a scenario where we want only parts of a page to change and other sections to be static as we move around a site. The static portion could represent a company logo or a menu, or a copyright statement. The dynamic part, on the other hand, has contents which change based on the interaction with a user. Here, for example, the contents in the dynamic part could reflect the menu option located in the static section of a page.

For practical realization of such a scenario where navigation of a site is important, frames are used. These subdivide a page so that different parts can contain either static or dynamic content, or both. Another benefit of frames is that only the dynamic content needs to be loaded each time. This should improve the download rate as compared to updating the complete page.

The purpose of this chapter, therefore, is to show how the Dreamweaver 4.0 environment supports the creation, editing and management of frames. In doing so, we will look at the tools and properties that facilitate setting-up frames for a site.

Understanding framesets

Each frame effectively contains an HTML file, or makes use of one or more HTML files. When working with frames, the frameset element is used to configure the page. In other words, framesets define the structure and attributes associated with a page. This would include information about the number of frames, their size, their contents and related attributes such as border thickness and colour, spacing between frames, etc. A frameset is, in fact, an HTML page which is invisible in a browser.

Framesets and, therefore, frames can be created within the Dreamweaver 4.0 environment either manually, or via the frameset option on the main menu, or through using predefined designs from the Objects panel. To manually insert a frameset, choose View | Visual Aids and then click on the Frame Borders option. Figure 8.1 depicts the scenario. This results in a (frame) border appearing around the edges of the page. Figure 8.2 gives an illustration of this. In order to create a frame, we simply drag a respective edge and drop it at a desired location on a page. This subdivides the page into two frames. Figure 8.3 provides an animated example of this, where the left edge is used to create the two frames. We can, of course, continue using this approach to produce more (vertical or horizontal) frames as required.

Alternatively, we can use the main menu option to generate a frameset. Choose Modify | Frameset and then either Split Frame Left, Right, Up, or Down. This results in the frame borders becoming visible and the respective frameset having two frames, split in the middle of the page. Figure 8.4 shows

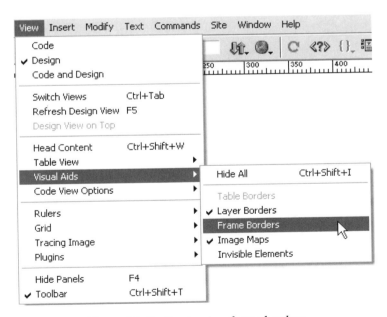

Figure 8.1 *Option to view frame borders.*

an example where the Split Frame Up option has been chosen. Note the readings on the vertical ruler. The origin here starts at the frame border.

Like in the first case, we can manually increase the size of a respective frame by using the size handles when the cursor is placed on a frame border. Click, drag and drop the border at a preferred location. To remove a frame border, select it and drag it off the page (or parent border, if nested frames are being used).

The third way of adding a frameset to a page is through the Objects panel. As Figure 8.5 depicts, we choose the category Frames. This opens up a number of predefined framesets. The frameset icons, which are then displayed on the Objects panel, are shown in Figure 8.6. Eight possible frameset combinations can be chosen. Each icon representing a frameset has a frame that is shown shaded (blue within the Dreamweaver 4.0 environment). This frame is used as a reference point for creating the other frame(s) for the combination. In other words, if we wanted to create a frame to the right side of an existing selected frame or page, then

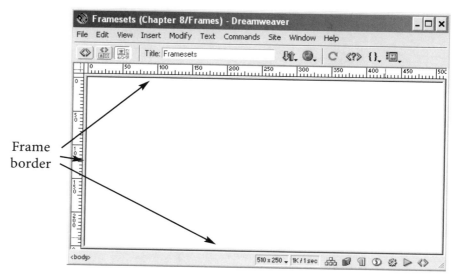

Figure 8.2 Frame border around the edges of a page.

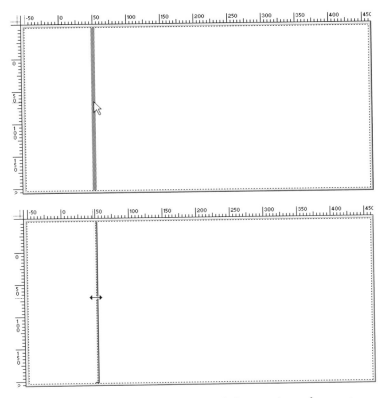

Figure 8.3 Drag and drop approach for creating a frameset.

the Right frameset (see Figure 8.6 for its location on the Objects panel) would be used. The white (unshaded) frame in each case points to a new frame (or frames) that will be generated.

We can add a predefined frameset, with reference to the current location of the insertion point, by using any one of the following three approaches:

- Click on the desired frameset icon on the Objects panel. A new frame (or frames) is produced with respect to the frame or page in which the insertion point resides; or
- Click, drag and drop the desired frameset icon on to an unselected frame. A new frame (or frames) is produced with respect to this (unselected) frame. This frame is also

used as a reference point for creating other frames in the frameset; or

- Choose `Insert | Frames` and then the required frameset from the submenu that opens. Figure 8.7 depicts the scenario, where we note that the eight combinations on the Objects panel form the options on the submenu.

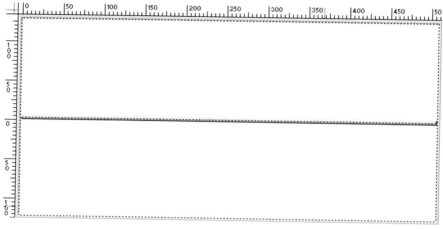

Figure 8.4 *Effect of choosing Split Frame Up option with* `Modify | Frameset`.

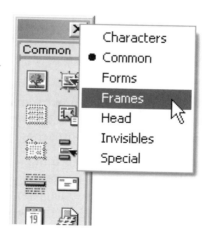

Figure 8.5 *Opening the Frames category on the Objects panel.*

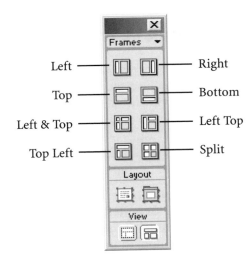

Figure 8.6 Objects panel showing available framesets.

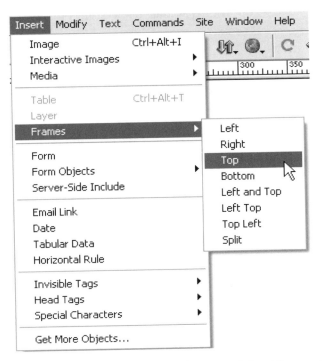

Figure 8.7 Using main menu to select a predefined frameset.

Creating nested framesets

Like nested layers, we can also have nested framesets. Here, a frameset is inserted into an existing frameset. This way, we can subdivide the area of a page into smaller sections, where each section is realized through a frame. Each occurrence of a frameset results in a corresponding file being created which comprises the information about the frameset (for example, the number of frames, frame border attributes, etc).

We may not have realized it, but we have already been working with nested framesets. If we look closely at some of the predefined framesets, then we can see that these use a nested combination for their realization. As an example, Figure 8.8 shows the Top and Top Left frameset icons available on the Objects panel. We can see the difference between the two framesets is that the bottom frame of the Top frameset has been split into two to yield Top Left frameset.

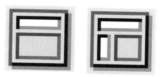

Figure 8.8 Top and Top Left frameset icons on Objects panel.

What in fact has happened is that the Top Left case makes use of two framesets: the first is similar to the Top frameset. This is the parent frameset in our example and it defines two (row) frames. The bottom frame is then split using another frameset, namely the Left frameset. This becomes the child frameset and comprises two (column) frames.

When nested framesets are used, we can insert additional frames by using the Alt key and then simply dragging the respective border to a desired position. Figure 8.9 depicts the scenario, where a new column frame has been added. If the Alt key was not used, then the respective frames will be resized when we drag and drop the frame border.

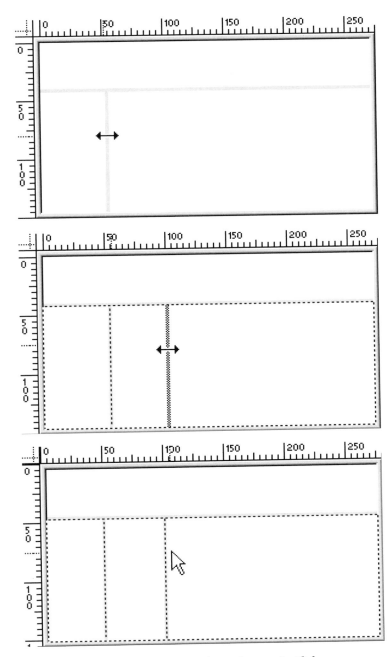

Figure 8.9 *Splitting an inner frame via Alt key.*

Using the frames panel

The Dreamweaver 4.0 environment supports a frames panel that gives a pictorial representation of the framesets and frames on the page. We can use the panel to select a desired frameset (or frame) and then view and edit its attributes, as required. To open the frames panel, do one of the following:

- Select Window | Frames; or
- Press and hold down the Shift key and then press function key F2.

The resulting panel is shown in Figure 8.10. In the example shown, the Top Left frameset is included on the page. Figure 8.11 shows the actual page contents, where text has been added to identify each frame.

Figure 8.10 The Frames panel.

As it stands, the frames panel is not really providing any additional assistance. If, however, we wanted next to include a Right frameset within the frame labelled in Figure 8.11 as Main, then the usefulness of the panel becomes a little clearer. We use the Objects panel to insert the Right frameset. The frames panel changes to reflect the insertion. As Figure 8.12 depicts, the panel shows a frameset with a thick border and frames as thin borders. From the panel, we can tell without too much difficulty that the page now consists of a nested (three) frameset structure.

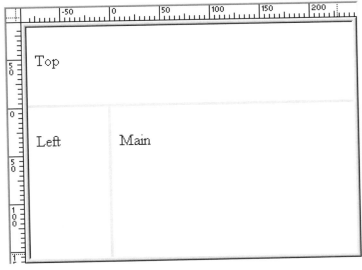

Figure 8.11 Top Left frameset on a page.

To select a frame, place the cursor within a frame on the Frames panel and click once. A selected frame, as Figure 8.13 shows, has a thin width border. A frameset can be selected by clicking on the desired frameset border. This results in thick width border to verify that the frameset has been selected.

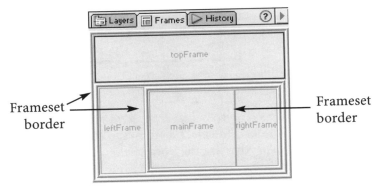

Figure 8.12 Frameset and frame borders on the frames panel.

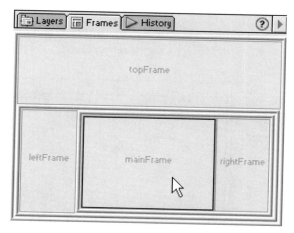

Figure 8.13 A selected frame on the frames panel.

Figure 8.14 depicts this case where the parent frameset is selected for the example mentioned above.

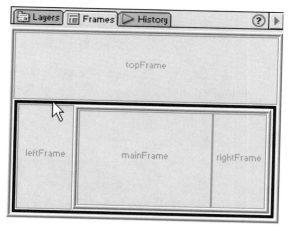

Figure 8.14 A selected frameset on the frames panel.

We can also select framesets and frames in the document window. To select a frameset, simply place the cursor on a respective frame border then click once. The respective frameset is selected. This is highlighted by dots appearing in the frame borders. Figure 8.15 depicts the scenario, where again the parent frameset is selected.

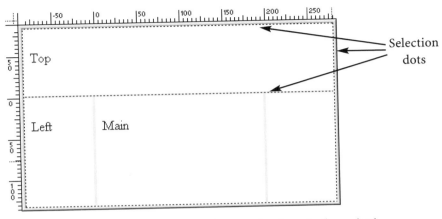

Figure 8.15 Dotted line indicates selection of a frame(set).

To select a frame, move the cursor within the desired frame on the page. Then press and hold the Alt key and click the mouse button once. The selected frame is highlighted with a dotted line (similar to a selected frameset, see Figure 8.15). We can also use a combination of the Alt key and the cursor (arrow) keys to change a selection. That is, if a frame is selected then by using this combination, we can broaden the selection to include other frames.

Using the frames properties panel

Once a frameset or a frame is selected, we can view and adjust their respective attributes. This is achieved through opening the Property Inspector panel, which in turn displays the attributes for the selection.

In the case of a frameset, as Figure 8.16 shows, we can change the colour and width of frame borders, as well as the dimensions for the frames within the frameset. The number of rows and columns within the frameset are listed on the left side of the panel. The dimensions within the Column (or Row) parameter refer to the frame that is shown in the RowCol Selection (located on the right side of the panel). In Figure 8.16, for example, the left frame has a width of 80 pixels. To

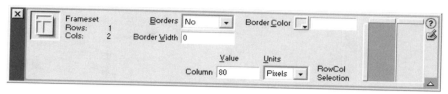

Figure 8.16 Property Inspector panel for a selected frameset.

view the dimensions of the right frame, click on the respective frame on the RowCol Selection. Units for the dimension are pixels, percent and relative. The percent refers to the size of the frameset, whilst relative can be used to fill space after frames using pixels and percent have been rendered.

To display border colours, we need to say Yes to the Borders parameter and then enter a non zero value for the Border Width. Choose (or enter a value for) a desired colour using the Border Color option. The choice of default for the Borders parameter allows a browser to decide how a border is displayed.

When a frame is selected, the Property Inspector panel can be used to modify a number of its attributes, including the name, margins, scrolling, resizing, and border parameters. The latter take precedence over any specified using the frameset properties.

Figure 8.17 shows the contents of the Property Inspector panel for a selected frame: we can modify the name of the frame by making use of the text associated with the Name Frame parameter. The frames panel will automatically be updated when a new name is entered. We can insert the path for the HTML file to be included in the frame through Src parameter. Either type the path in the text box, or use the file icon to browse to a file, or click and dynamically attach a file by using the point-to-file icon. We can also insert a file by means of the main menu. In this case, place the insertion point within the frame and then choose File | Open in Frame to browse for a desired file.

In addition, we can refer to an external site, so that when the browser displays the frame, it downloads the intended web page. In this case, simply enter the URL in the text box

✕		Frame Name		Src	/Chapter 8/Panel.htm		⊕ ▢	Borders	Default ▾	②
	▢	mainFrame		Scroll	Default ▾	☐ No Resize	Border Color ▢			
		Margin Width								
		Margin Height							▲	

Figure 8.17 Property Inspector panel for a selected frame.

associated with Src parameter on the Property Inspector panel. As Figure 8.18 shows, the Dreamweaver 4.0 environment acknowledges the URL by placing a message in the selected frame. When the browser renders this, it will download the web page from the mentioned remote site and use this as content for the frame.

Frames can have (horizontal and vertical) scroll bars appended to them, if the contents are bigger than the size of the frame. With the Scroll parameter, we have four options:

- Yes. Attach scroll bars irrespective of content size.
- No. Do not attach scroll bars. If content is larger than the frame size, the viewer has no way of accessing it.
- Auto. Dynamically turn on either or both scroll bars if the content is larger than the frame. Otherwise, show no scroll bars.
- Default. Allow browser to choose most appropriate option. This normally is Auto.

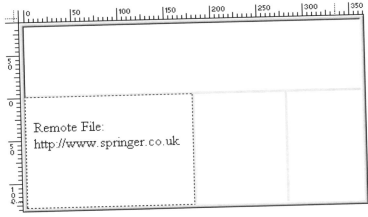

Figure 8.18 Frame message highlighting remote file usage.

The No Resize parameter when checked precludes viewers from changing the frame size. Otherwise, the viewer is able to select the border of a frame, in a browser, and drag it to change its size. This can be advantageous as it may make the page more readable, though a well-designed site will not require manual layout changes when viewed.

Frames can have their border colour defined through using the Border Color parameter on the Property Inspector panel. For this to be visible, choose the Yes option from the pull-down menu for Borders. A border can be made invisible by choosing the No option, though this depends on the settings of adjacent frames and the defining frameset. These should also have a No for Borders, or have the parent frameset setting to No and the adjacent frames to Default for Borders. Any border colours defined for a frame take precedence over a similar setting made by a defining frameset.

If we wanted to change the background colour or even insert a background image to a frame, then place the insertion point in the frame and choose `Modify | Page Properties`. This opens the Page Properties dialogue box. As Figure 8.19 manifests, enter path or browse for a file which will be used for the background for the Background Image setting, or use Background to set a preferred background colour.

The Margin Width and Margin Height specify, in pixels, the size of any spacing between the frame borders and its content. Margin Width establishes the left and right margins, whilst Margin Height sets the top and bottom margins.

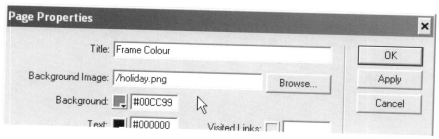

Figure 8.19 Setting background attributes for a frame.

Using links for frame content

One of the key roles that framesets and frames play is that they allow one frame to control the content of another. In such a scenario, the two frames need to be linked so that choosing a menu option in one frame, for example, results in the other frame opening the relevant page (or site). This is realized, in practice, by defining a target frame for the link, so that when the viewer selects some linked text, the target frame opens with the outcome.

As discussed in Chapter 6, we can link elements on a page to others on the same or different page, or even to a remote site. What we want to do here is to define the target frame. This can be achieved through the Property Inspector panel for a hyperlinked text or image (refer to Chapter 6 for information on this). When the panel is opened for the linked element, use the Target parameter to specify where the linked file should open. Typically, we have four options:

- `_blank` opens a new browser window and displays the linked page.
- `_parent` opens the linked page in the parent frameset. If not nested, the page will be displayed in the browser window.
- `_self` is the default setting that opens the linked page in the current window or frame.
- `_top` opens the linked page in the browser window, replacing contents of frames.

When we add framesets and frames to a page, the Target parameter also includes the names of the frames as part of its list. We can then choose to make any of the frames as targets for a hyperlink. Figure 8.20 depicts the scenario, where the four frames shown in the frames panel are listed within the pop-down menu associated with the Target parameter.

Saving framesets and frames

We will need to save both framesets and frames before they can be viewed in a browser. When framesets and frames are created within the Dreamweaver 4.0 environment, they are automatically given temporary filenames such as UntitledFrameset-3 and UntitledFrame-5. These suggestive names appear when we want to save. Clearly, it is best to change these to reflect the contents and to assist in recognizing the same.

In order to save a frameset or a frame, we must first select them. Here, the Frames panel or the document window can be used as discussed earlier in this chapter. For a selected frameset, choose File | Save Frameset As. This opens

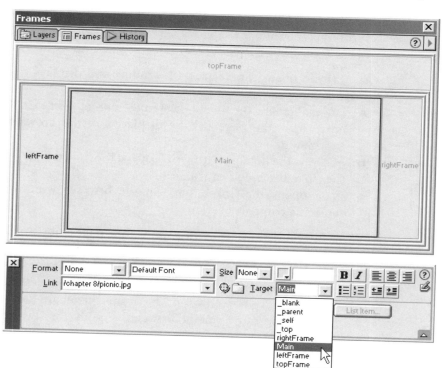

Figure 8.20 Choosing a frame as target for a hyperlinked page.

the Save As dialogue box. Enter a desired name for the frameset. It may be wise to develop a strategy for naming framesets (and frames) early on in a development since it can become tedious to distinguish between different framesets, and between framesets and frames. This is because both are saved as HTML files. Using 'fs' in the name to signify a frameset, for example, could be useful. Once a frameset has been saved, we can then use `File | Save Frameset` to store updates.

The saving process for frames is similar to that outlined for framesets. In this case, place the insertion point inside a desired frame and then choose `File | Save Frameset As` initially, followed by `File | Save` for updates. In addition, we can use `File | Save All Frames` to save both frames and framesets. The way this works is to open respective Save As dialogue boxes in a sequence so that desired file names can be entered. As a dialogue box is opened, the document window is updated to highlight the selected frame (or frameset).

Chapter
9

Working with HTML and JavaScript

Introduction

We have thus far used the visual form of the Dreamweaver 4.0 environment to design and create a page. We can continue with this practice to gain sophisticated web pages and sites. When we use the design view to develop a page, HTML and scripting is being added in the background. The browser does not work with the visual form, but with HTML to render and display our pages. There are times where it may be more convenient to work with HTML rather than the visual environment. This enables more control over the way a page is presented and can be used for debugging and for troubleshooting.

As we will learn in this chapter, there are a number of tools that enable us to work with the background code to a page. These allow HTML codes (and scripts) to be viewed, edited and cleaned-up. The Dreamweaver 4.0 environment also supports the usage of external HTML editors. This means that code can be created either within the Dreamweaver 4.0 environment or in an external text editor, and then be exchanged between two applications.

The chapter also shows how to work with JavaScript within the environment and what features are available to assist in generating, editing and debugging scripts. In the case of the latter, the on-board debugger can be used to check code for errors.

The focus of discussion here is on the development tools available and not on learning HTML or JavaScript. However, as we will see, having both visual and textual versions of a page can help in understanding the workings of both HTML and JavaScript.

Understanding HTML

To gain a better understanding of how the Dreamweaver 4.0 environment supports working with HTML, let us quickly review some basic aspects of HTML. The letters HTML stand for HyperText Markup Language and provide a means of assisting the browser in the way a page should be displayed. The page, itself, is written as plain text and tags are added to tell the browser how to render the text.

If, for example, we wanted to emphasize a word on a page, then we could italicize, underline, change font size, or make it bold. To express the latter in HTML, we make use of the `<b>` tag. When the browser encounters this in the HTML document, it starts to make every word bold, until it comes across the closing tag, `</b>`. When the browser sees the forward slash (/) within a tag, it reverts to the previous state.

HTML makes use of a number of tags. These are used for text styling, image insertion and presentation, table and list generation, frame production, form creation, hyperlink formation, etc. Most tags have specific attributes which enable further control of how an element should be displayed. For example, `<p font align=center>` uses the align attribute to centre justify the text belonging to the paragraph tag. Likewise, other tags have their respective attributes. A tag can make use of more than one attribute at a time.

An HTML document works with two sections: namely, the head and body. The head typically contains tags relating to the browser title bar, status line, style sheet information, etc; whilst the body provides the contents of page. As manifested in Figure 9.1, a HTML page requires certain basic tags. These include `<html>` which tells the browser to expect HTML codes, `<head>` and `<body>`. For more information on HTML and dynamic HTML, see Essential Dynamic HTML *fast*, by Aladdin Ayesh, published by Springer-Verlag.

The design view for the Dreamweaver 4.0 environment can replicate the two sections for an HTML document. That is, that we can choose to view the design in terms of a head and a body. To do this, select `View | Head Content`. Figure 9.2 gives an illustrative example for the HTML code shown in Figure 9.1. To view the contents of any items in the head content, we make use of the Property Inspector panel. As

```
<html>

<head>
<title>HTML Basics</title>
</head>

<body>
<p> This is plain text, written
using a paragraph tag.
</p>
</body>

</html>
```

Figure 9.1 *Sample HTML page.*

Figure 9.3 depicts, click on the item of interest (in our basic example, only the title element is in the head section) to view its attributes in the panel.

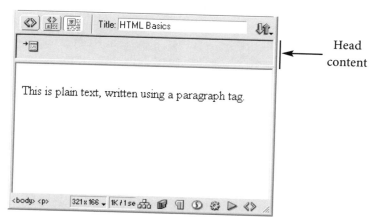

Head content

Figure 9.2 *Head and body sections of a page, in design view.*

Figure 9.3 Viewing attributes of a (selected) head content item

Viewing HTML code

The Dreamweaver 4.0 environment provides a number of ways of viewing and editing HTML codes. As mentioned in Chapter 1, we can work in design (visual) view only, code view only, or with both views. As Figure 9.4 shows, we can make use of the main menu to select any one of these options. Choose View and then either Code, Design, or Code and Design. Figure 9.5 gives an illustrative example of each, where the page contains a single image (star.png). Since the image in the figure is selected, the corresponding HTML code is highlighted.

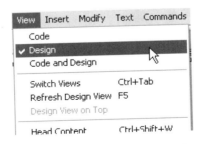

Figure 9.4 Choosing an editing mode for a page.

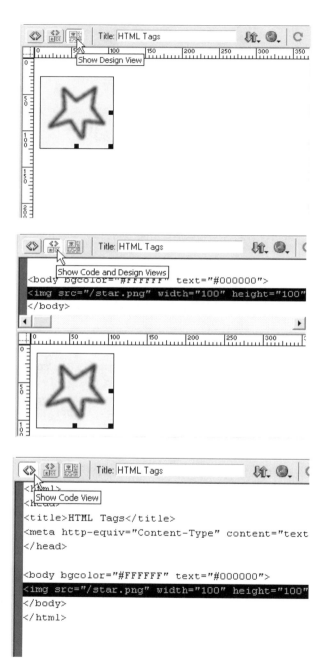

Figure 9.5 Available views of a page.

When the option to display both views is turned on, we can toggle between the two by either using View | Switch Views, or through a combination of the control (CTRL) and the Tab key. This in turn selects the view for editing purposes. In addition, we can also click within the desired view to make it active.

In Figure 9.5, the design view is shown to occupy the bottom half of the window when both views are selected. If we preferred, we can swap the views around by selecting View | Design View on Top. This will place the contents of the design view on the top half of the window. In addition, we can adjust the height of each half by selecting and dragging the splitter bar to a desired location. Figure 9.6 depicts the scenario.

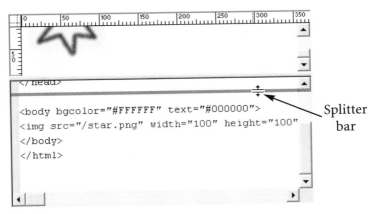

Splitter bar

Figure 9.6 Splitter bar being used to adjust view heights.

Editing HTML code

We can create and edit HTML documents when the code view option is active. Simply use the resulting window (half window if shared with design view) as a text editor. Some common HTML tags can be inserted using the Text submenu. As Figure 9.7 shows, this is located on the main menu and has several options which can assist a designer. In addition, the context menu provides further editing options. Whilst within the code view window, right click to open the context menu. The menu (and therefore the options) is shown in Figure 9.8.

When changes are made to the source code, they are usually not updated within the design view until both views are synchronized. We can synchronize the views by any of the following four ways:

- Click within the Design view window after editing HTML code; or
- Choose View | Refresh Design View; or
- Press function key F5; or
- Use the Refresh button on the toolbar. If the toolbar is not open, then choose View | Toolbar. The position of the Refresh button on the toolbar is highlighted in Figure 9.9.

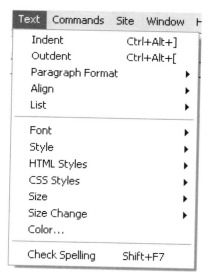

Figure 9.7 Text submenu, located on the main menu.

Instead of viewing and editing HTML within the code view window, we can use a separate window to do the same. This window is referred to as the code inspector. The code inspector does not offer any additional editing (or viewing) options. However, being a separate window, it does offer the

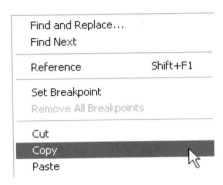

Figure 9.8 Context menu when using code view.

convenience of working in design view and being able to assess the HTML code at the same time.

We can open the code inspector by either using the main menu or via the launcher bar. In the case of the former, choose Window | Code Inspector. This acts as a toggle to open and close the code inspector. To use the launcher bar, simply click on the corresponding button to open (and close) the code inspector. Figure 9.10 shows the location of the button on the launcher bar. Alternatively, we can use the function key F10 to do the same. An illustration of the resulting code inspector is given in Figure 9.11.

The code inspector has a toolbar at the top. The tools featured on this are also available on the main toolbar (associated

Refresh button

Figure 9.9 Refresh button on the toolbar.

Show Code Inspector

Figure 9.10 Code inspector option on the launcher bar.

with the document window). The six tools available are shown in Figure 9.12. The primary tool here is the View options, which covers options related to the (HTML) code displayed by the inspector. The five options it offers, which are available on the pull-down menu, are shown in Figure 9.13. These can be summarized as follows:

- Word Wrap. Moves the code onto the next line, so that horizontal scrolling is not required.
- Line Numbers. Shows line numbers on the left (blue) margin. Useful for debugging, especially when working with JavaScript.
- Highlight Invalid HTML. As the name suggests, any HTML tags or statements which are not recognized are highlighted.
- Syntax Coloring. HTML statements are coloured to provide a clearer presentation of code. More on code colours in the next section.
- Auto Indent. Automatically indents code, with reference to the preference settings. The latter is discussed in the following section.

An illustrative example of the working of these view options is shown in Figure 9.14. In the example, all the five mentioned

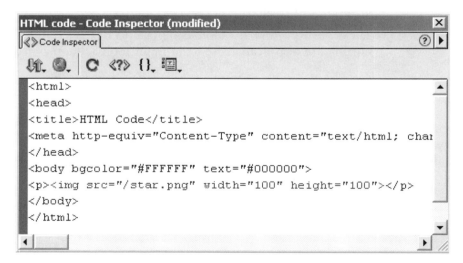

Figure 9.11 The code inspector.

view options are active. Therefore, line numbers for each HTML statement are shown, text code is word wrapped, HTML code is being checked for errors (line 8), and syntax is colour coded (line 7). The Auto Indent option is active, though in the example shown it does not require this. As mentioned earlier, we must refresh the display for the environment to recognize any changes in the code.

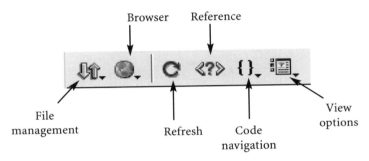

Figure 9.12 Toolbar on the code inspector.

When an HTML tag or statement is highlighted as being invalid, a corresponding message appears when it is selected whilst in design view. The Property Inspector panel invokes the message, which in turn identifies the reasons for the invalidity and probable solutions. Figure 9.15 depicts the case for the example code (line 8) shown in Figure 9.14.

There are other features that the Dreamweaver 4.0 environment has which assist in creating and editing HTML elements. This includes a Quick Tag Editor, which becomes available when in design view. Open the Property Inspector panel and click the corresponding icon, located on the right

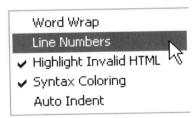

Figure 9.13 Menu for View options, on code inspector.

```
1  <html>
2  <head>
3  <title>HTML Code</title>
4  <meta http-equiv="Content-Type"
   content="text/html; charset=iso-8859-1">
5  </head>
6  <body bgcolor="#FFFFFF" text="#000000">
7  <p><img src="/star.png" width="100"
   height="100"></p>
8  <font face="arial"> Great fun
9  </body>
10 </html>
11
```

Figure 9.14 Example HTML using code view options.

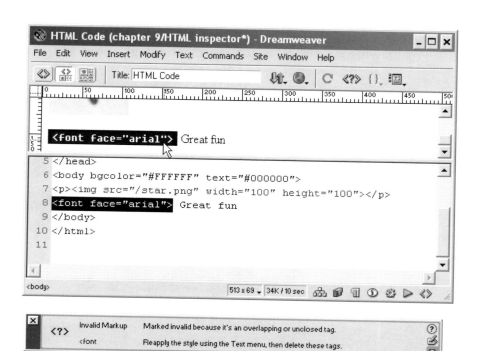

Figure 9.15 Invalid HTML message on Property Inspector panel.

side of the panel. Figure 9.16 depicts the scenario. An example of the workings of the editor is shown in Figure 9.17. Here, we are inserting a table element. As the table tag has been written, the editor automatically returns a list of possible attributes that could be used. If we wanted to edit existing HTML statements, we simply place the insertion point within the desired statement and open the editor. The complete HTML statement will appear in the editor for adjustment.

Figure 9.16 Opening the Quick Tag Editor.

When working with a large HTML document, it becomes difficult to keep track of all the tags so that modifications, if required, can be made. The Dreamweaver 4.0 environment provides a hierarchical list on the launcher bar to assist the designer. This is visible when in design view. Figure 9.18 provides an illustrative example. The list should be read from left to right, with the tag that is shown bold being the one currently selected. This, in Figure 9.18, is <tr>, which in turn results in the respective table row contents being selected. If we then wanted to edit the tag, we make use of the context menu and select Edit Tag to open the Quick Tag Editor. Figure 9.19 depicts the scenario where the context menu has been used to open the editor.

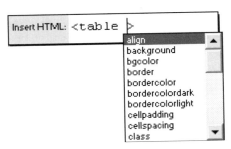

Figure 9.17 Using the Quick Tag Editor.

Hierarchical
HTML tag list

Figure 9.18 *HTML tag list on the launcher bar.*

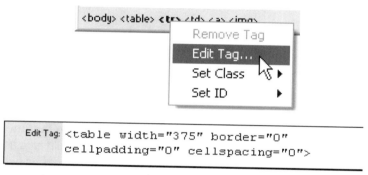

Figure 9.19 *Opening Quick Tag Editor via launcher bar.*

Setting code preferences

Dreamweaver 4.0 environment provides a number of options for presenting (HTML) code. In fact, there are three separate preference panels: one for colours, one for formatting and the other for rewriting code. These are available via the preferences dialogue box, which can be opened by choosing Edit | Preferences. The three panels of concern here are available through the Category option. These are shown in Figure 9.20.

The Code Colors category controls the way text, including HTML tags, are colour coded when displayed in code view or within the code inspector. As Figure 9.21 (also Plate XV) shows, we can set colours for tags, the text between tags,

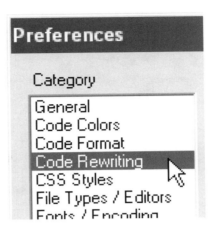

Figure 9.20 *Code options on the preferences dialogue box.*

comments, etc. The Tag Specific section allows tags to be individually colour coded. Choose default (as per Tag Default parameter) or select a desired colour. The text between the tags can be set to have the same (new) colour as the tags by checking the box associated with Apply Color to Tag Colors parameter.

To control the way HTML text will be displayed, we make use of the Code Format category. This, as shown in Figure 9.22, has options for setting indent in general and specifically for tags used to represent tables and cells, and framesets and frames. In addition, we can specify word-wrap at specific line lengths; choose the type of line breaks to use and whether to use lowercase or uppercase for tags and attributes. The Override Case Of parameter controls whether to apply the case options or not. Check the boxes if you want Dreamweaver 4.0 environment to follow the default case settings for tags and attributes. Finally, choose either DIV or CENTER to specify the tag to be used for centring objects.

The settings made in the Code Format category are applicable to new pages that are created. To use the same settings on new documents, open the document and then choose `Commands | Apply Source Formatting`.

The third set of options for working with HTML code is available via the Code Rewriting category. The purpose of

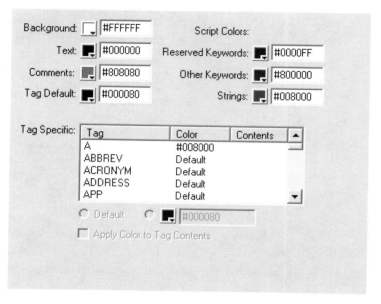

Figure 9.21 *Code colour settings on preferences dialogue box (also Plate XV).*

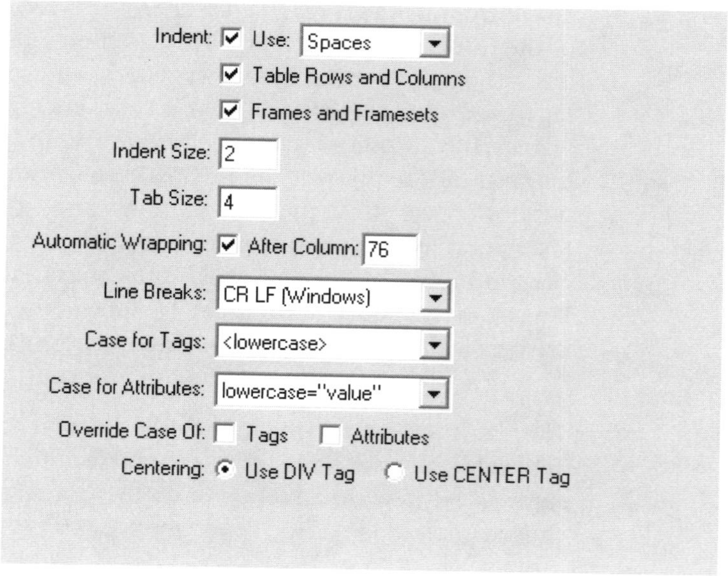

Figure 9.22 *Code format options on preferences dialogue box.*

these settings is to control the way the Dreamweaver 4.0 environment opens a page. The available options are shown in Figure 9.23, which to some degree are self-explanatory. The warning option returns a message showing problems with the code that requires correction. It is worth noting also that the Never Rewrite Code option is best left checked since it prevents the environment from changing the code, which may be correct, but it does not recognize.

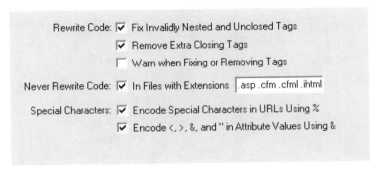

Figure 9.23 *Code Rewriting panel on preferences dialogue box.*

Adding JavaScript

We may not have realized it since we have primarily focused on using the design view for our development, but we have already employed JavaScript to create effects such as mouse rollovers. By its name, we can tell that it is a scripting language, which allows dynamic pages to be generated to run on the client-side.

Dreamweaver 4.0 supports the embodiment of scripts in a design through a variety of ways. We can create, edit, insert and debug scripts. Although the environment can work with other types of scripts (such as VBScripts), we will centre on JavaScript as the prime example.

To create a script for a document, first turn on the option to show script markers so that when a script is added, we have knowledge of it when in design view. Choose `View | Visual Aids` and then Invisible Elements to show all elements that are classified as invisible (such as markers) by the environment. Then, follow the steps outlined below:

- Position the insertion point where the script is to be added.
- Either choose `Insert | Invisible Tags` and then Script, or use the Objects panel. In the latter case, and as shown by Figure 9.24, choose Invisibles as the category. Then click on the Script icon. Figure 9.25 depicts the scenario.

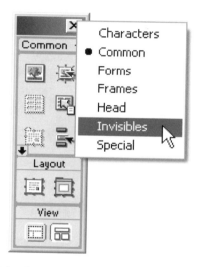

Figure 9.24 *Selecting Invisibles category for the Objects panel.*

- A dialogue box similar to that shown in Figure 9.26 is then invoked. The Language parameter has four options: JavaScript, JavaScript1.1, JavaScript1.2 and VBScript. Choose JavaScript.
- Write the required script in the Content text box.
- Press OK when the desired script has been written. The script is then added at the specified insertion point.

Figure 9.27 gives an illustrative example where an empty JavaScript has been added to the page. The script in design

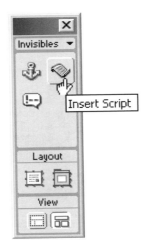

Figure 9.25 Choosing Script option on the Objects panel.

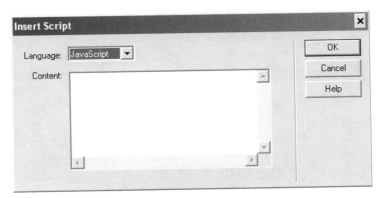

Figure 9.26 Dialogue box for adding a script to a page.

view takes the form of a marker, whilst the `script` tags are included in code view.

We can make use of the Property Inspector panel to create a script or to insert an external script file. In fact, when the panel is open in code view, its contents reflect those for normal text. In other words, HTML code is treated like any other text. The panel, however, changes for a script: place the insertion point on any part of the script to activate the

Property Inspector panel in script mode. Figure 9.28 shows the resulting panel.

Script marker

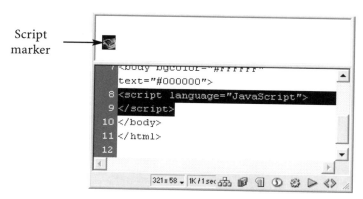

Figure 9.27 *Insertion of a (blank) script on the page.*

Figure 9.28 *Property Inspector panel for a script.*

We can edit to modify the script that has the insertion point in it, or edit to create a new script through using the Edit button on the panel. Alternatively, the folder icon associated with the Source parameter can be used to browse for an external script file. The Edit button, in fact, opens up the Script Properties dialogue box. This, as Figure 9.29 shows, also has the option of including an external script file to the page.

The Assets panel can be used to keep a track of external scripts. Choose Window | Assets or press function key F11 to open the panel. As Figure 9.30 shows, select the Scripts category to view external script files for the whole site or those specified as favourites. The files listed are only those that are externally created with a corresponding extension (such as 'js' for JavaScript). Typically, a script is added to the

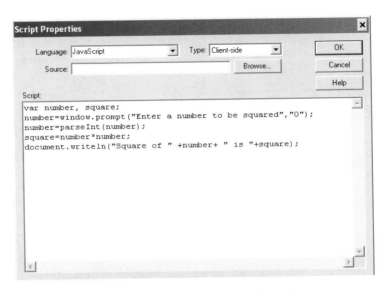

Figure 9.29 *Script Properties dialogue box.*

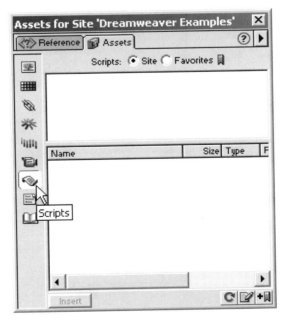

Figure 9.30 *Assets panel set to show (external) scripts.*

head section of a page and we can achieve this by selecting the desired script from the Assets panel and dragging it into the head content (when the page is in design view).

Supporting code features

Other useful features, which support working with code, include the option to check for missing or extra tags in the case of HTML and braces for scripts. Braces, that is { and }, are included in scripts (and other programming paradigms) to specify the scope of a code statement. Typical usage for

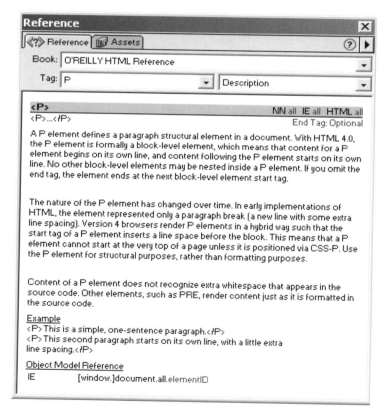

Figure 9.31 The References panel.

these includes control loops and conditional (if and else) scenarios. To initiate checking, choose `Edit | Select Parent Tag` for HTML tags and `Edit | Balance Braces` for scripts.

To get information on a tag, or an attribute, or a JavaScript object, the References panel can be used. This can be opened through the toolbar (see Figure 9.12) or by choosing `Window | Reference`. The panel typically includes, as Figure 9.31 manifests, a brief description and an example. In addition, the attributes associated with the tag can also be displayed. These are available by means of the pull down menu that appears to the right of a tag (or an object) menu. We can either open the panel and choose our reference query, or select a tag or an object and then activate the panel. In case of the latter, the panel will open with information on the selected element.

Dreamweaver 4.0 also has a number of additional features that allow us to debug code, in particular JavaScript. We will be looking at the built-in debugger that is available in Chapter 11.

Chapter 10

Working with Style Sheets and Forms

Introduction

As our web site develops, we would want to control better the way the content of each page is presented within a browser. The goal would be to achieve uniformity in presentation across the pages so that headings, text, image captions, tables, etc, have respectively similar appearance. We commonly gain this through using styles. The attraction of using styles is that if we wanted to change the appearance of our site, we modify only the defining style sheet. This in turn will result in the document being reformatted using the change set of style attributes without any further editing to page content. The Dreamweaver 4.0 environment supports both HTML styles and Cascading Style Sheets (CSS). We will look at both types in this chapter.

The other main thrust of this chapter is the creation and usage of forms. These play a critical role for a site since they can be used to gather information about the viewer, their interests, their requirements, or simply to get feedback about the products offered on the site. The chapter will show how we can use the tools provided by the Dreamweaver 4.0 environment to quickly generate forms for our web site.

We will start our discussion by looking at HTML styles and then move onto CSS. Having done this, we will then have covered all the key components that allow for the creation of a site. The only aspect to add to the site would be a (feedback) form, which we look at in the latter part of this chapter.

Creating HTML styles

The HTML styles allow for formatting of text through the application of basic HTML tags such as `<b>`, `<i>`, `<centre>`, and `<font>`. Tags can be used as a combination to define a style. We make use of the HTML Styles panel for creating and applying a desired style. To open the panel, either choose `Window | HTML Styles`, or use the corresponding icon on the launcher bar. Figure 10.1 shows the latter case, where the icon acts as a toggle to open or close the panel.

Figure 10.1 HTML Styles icon on the launcher bar.

The resulting HTML styles panel that opens is depicted in Figure 10.2 (also Plate XV). As the figure shows, there are several parts to the panel: if we wanted to create a new style, we can click on the New Style button, or use the context menu either the one shown or through right clicking whilst on the panel. In the latter case, and as Figure 10.3 illustrates, we then choose New to open the corresponding dialogue box. Alternatively, we can make use of the main menu by selecting Text | HTML Styles and then New Style.

As Figure 10.4 shows, there are a number of options for defining a new (or modifying an existing) style: the Name parameter allows for labelling the style and is used in the panel list. We then have a choice through Apply To parameter

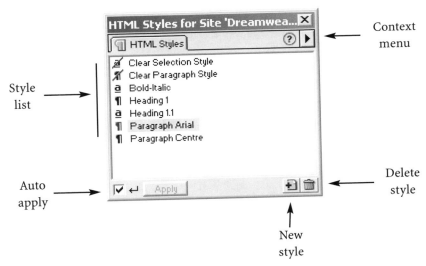

Figure 10.2 HTML Styles panel (also Plate XV).

Figure 10.3 Option to create a new style via context menu.

whether to apply the style to a selection (for example, a word or a sentence) or to a paragraph. In the case of the latter, the style affects the entire paragraph in which the insertion point resides. The When Applying option determines how the HTML styles work with any applicable, primarily, CSS for the

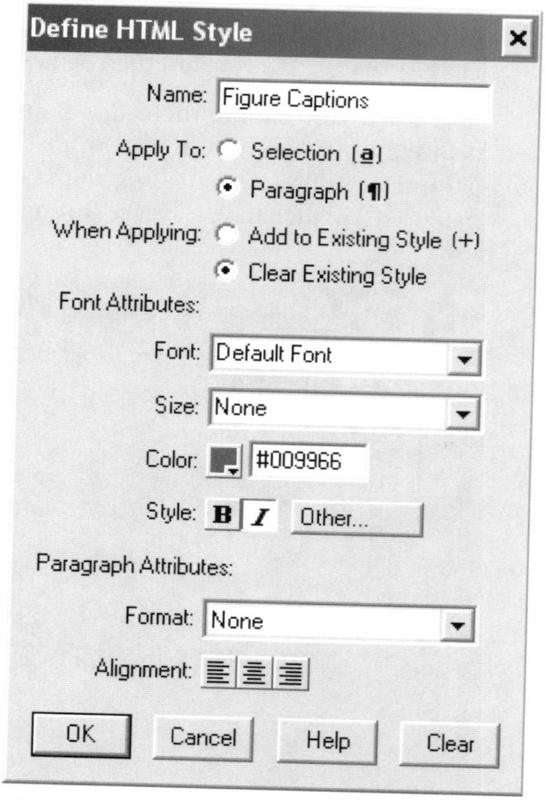

Figure 10.4 Define HTML Style dialogue box.

selection or paragraph. We have the choice to either add the defining style to any existing style (CSS or HTML), or to override these with the new style. The remaining option allows for defining the formatting for the style.

We can open an existing style by selecting the Edit option from the context menu (see Figure 10.3) or via Text | HTML Styles and then the desired style from the submenu. This results in the Define HTML Style dialogue box (similar to Figure 10.4) opening with the original formatting options selected. Any changes made to the style content are not automatically reflected in the text on the page that was using the style.

To use an existing style, we make use of the Auto apply section (see Figure 10.2 (also Plate XV)). Here, if the Auto apply checkbox is selected, then click on the desired style once. If, on the other hand, the Auto apply checkbox is not selected, then click the desired style and then the Apply button.

The top two items listed in the HTML Styles panel are not styles themselves. They are, in fact, options for removing text styling respectively from a paragraph or a selection. Both options work on HTML styles and changes made through the Property Inspector panel. They do not affect CSS formatting.

Understanding CSS

HTML styles provide a simple way of understanding how styles can be applied to a page. Their main shortcoming, however, is that they are only applicable to selected text. Even then, if the style is updated, the corresponding text using the style is left unchanged. One can work with such an arrangement on a small scale, but it is impractical with organizational web sites where a significant number of pages of content are common.

CSS (cascading style sheets) offer a solution to this difficulty. With CSS, all formatting styles are available for single or multiple documents. Moreover, if a CSS style is modified, this is automatically reflected in all the documents using the respective style. CSS also offer control over more attributes, such as bullet points, than HTML styles.

As we will see, CSS styles are labelled through a desired name or by the corresponding HTML tag (whose attributes have been defined). We can work with basic text formats or develop unique HTML attributes such as mouse rollover effects. In the case of text styling, for example, we may want to specify the attributes (such as face, size, or colour) for the font element. The effect of this would be that wherever the font tag is used in the document, it would make use of the defined CSS style. There is an exception, however, when there is a conflict between CSS or HTML styles, the latter takes precedence.

Creating a HTML tag style

The quickest way to get going with CSS is to create a style sheet for a HTML tag. We start with opening the corresponding panel by choosing Window | CSS Styles. Figure 10.5 shows the resulting panel, where we note that this is similar to HTML Styles panel apart from the two labelled options.

We need then to choose the option to create a new CSS style. There are three ways of doing this, either choose Text | CSS Styles and then New Style, or click the button on the panel (with a cross, located at bottom right), or use the context menu to select New Style. The latter option is shown in Figure 10.6. This opens the New Style dialogue box, an illustrative example of which is given in Figure 10.7.

The key option on the New Style panel is Type, which specifies the CSS style. At this stage, we want to work with a HTML tag, so select Redefine HTML Tag. The Name parameter, as Figure 10.8 shows, then provides a list of tags to select. Choose 'p' (for paragraph). We can also type the name of the tag in the respective text box and then press OK.

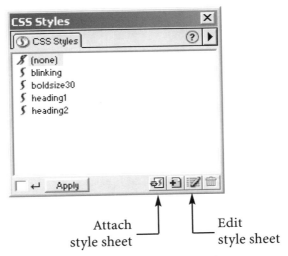

Attach
style sheet

Edit
style sheet

Figure 10.5 CSS Styles panel.

We are now in a position to define what the new style (for 'p') will be, through the resulting dialogue box that opens. Figure 10.9 depicts this for our example. As this shows, there are eight categories to choose from. Each category has a set of specific options that allow a desired effect to be realized. We note in Figure 10.9 that some attributes cannot be displayed within the Dreamweaver 4.0 environment. In fact, some earlier browser versions will also not be in a position to display certain attributes. In addition, Internet Explorer and Netscape Navigator will display some attributes differently. The attributes that cannot be displayed by the Dreamweaver

Figure 10.6 Option for a new CSS style, via context menu.

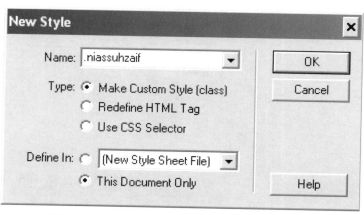

Figure 10.7 New Style dialogue box for CSS case.

4.0 environment are shown with an asterisk (*) appended to their name.

We make use of the Type category to add a style to the 'p' tag. In our example, the defining attributes that are used are as follows:

- Font: Geneva, Arial, Helvetica, san-serif
- Size: 36
- Weight: Bold
- Color: #FF0000 (red)

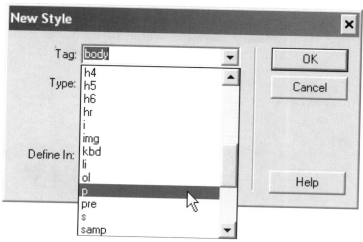

Figure 10.8 Choosing a HTML tag for a new CSS style.

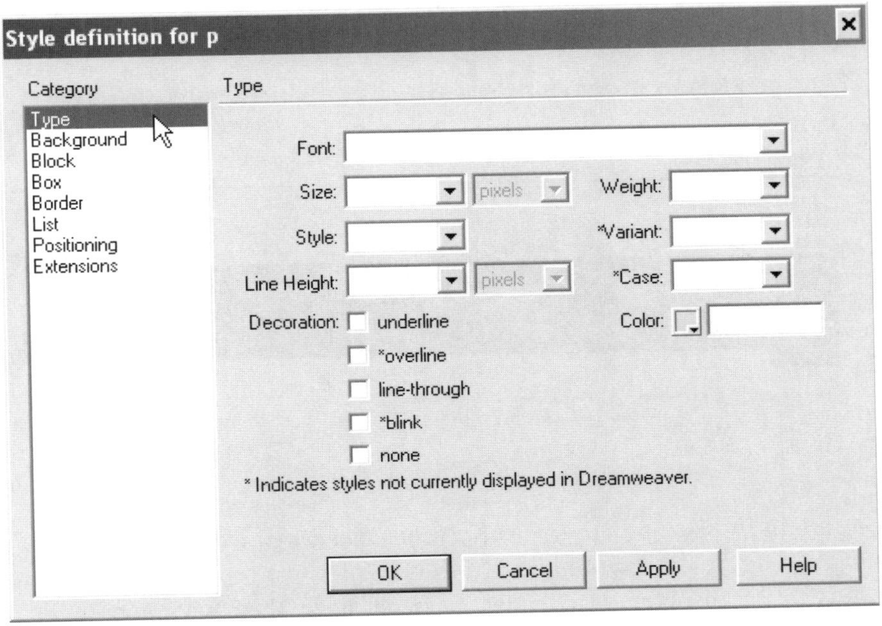

Figure 10.9 Style Definition dialogue box (for 'p').

When these values have been entered, click Apply or OK. Any text on the document page making use of the tag (unless locally styled) will automatically be changed to reflect the new style. For HTML tag styles, no entry is made in the CSS Styles panel. The styles are applicable as they are used on a page.

When a style is created, it is automatically placed in the head section of a page. As Figure 10.10 (also Plate XVI) manifests, the style and its attributes are displayed when in code view. In fact, the attributes can also be edited here without further reference to the CSS Styles panel. Any changes that are made manually, however, are automatically registered on the Style Definition dialogue box.

Figure 10.10 (also Plate XVI) shows how we can select the desired style through the head content (choose View | Head Content to open). Looking closely at Figure 10.10 (also Plate XVI), we note that comment tags are used to nest in the style tag. The purpose of these is to prevent older browsers from

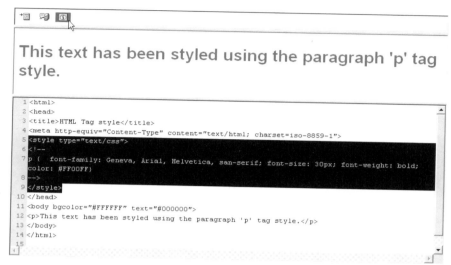

```
 1 <html>
 2 <head>
 3 <title>HTML Tag style</title>
 4 <meta http-equiv="Content-Type" content="text/html; charset=iso-8859-1">
 5 <style type="text/css">
 6 <!--
 7 p {  font-family: Geneva, Arial, Helvetica, san-serif; font-size: 30px; font-weight: bold;
    color: #FF00FF)
 8 -->
 9 </style>
10 </head>
11 <body bgcolor="#FFFFFF" text="#000000">
12 <p>This text has been styled using the paragraph 'p' tag style.</p>
13 </body>
14 </html>
15
```

Figure 10.10 _Selecting a style via head content, in design view (also Plate XVI)._

displaying an error message since they may not be in a position to render the style. In addition, each attribute uses a colon (:) to separate its name and its corresponding value. A semi-colon (;) separates the attributes themselves. We can make use of this when manually editing the style contents in code view (or via the code inspector).

Creating a customized CSS style

Instead of using a HTML style, we can create a CSS style to meet some design requirements. This is particularly useful where different styles are applied at different places within a site. We can customize to suit and meet our requirements. The process for creating a customized style is similar to that discussed in the previous section for HTML styles.

We start by opening the CSS Styles panel (choose Window | CSS Styles). This time, we select Make Custom Style (class) for the Type option (see Figure 10.7). We will then need to enter a name for the style. The following convention is used for the name:

- Start with a period (.). Dreamweaver 4.0 automatically enters this if we failed to add this on.
- Next must follow a character (not a number).
- No spaces or any other special characters are allowed for a name.
- .bigtext, .bolditalics5, .myStyle23, etc, are all acceptable.

Having given the CSS style a name, we are now ready to define the style attributes. Press OK on the panel to open the Style Definition dialogue box. The contents of this dialogue box are the same as discussed in the previous section.

Let's assume we want to use the Background category to add a background image to a selection on our page. Figure 10.11 shows the panel for the Background category. We use the Background Image parameter to specify the path to our desired background image. The options on the panel allow us to tailor the image to meet our requirements: Repeat controls how the image is tiled; Attachment allows the image to either be fixed or scroll with the image; and Horizontal Position and Vertical Position set the respective initial positions for the image. For our CSS style (.bkimage), we make the settings shown in Figure 10.12 and then press OK. The new style then appears within the CSS Styles panel, as well as on the submenu of Text | CSS Styles.

Once a style is defined, it is applied to the document page in a similar manner to that discussed for HTML styles: place the insertion point within the text to which the CSS style is to be applied and then choose either the main menu or the CSS Styles panel to select the style. With the former, choose Text | CSS Styles and then the desired style from the resulting submenu. The panel provides two ways of applying a style: select the Auto apply option (see Figure 10.2 (also Plate XV)) and then click on the style from the list provided, or click on the style first and then press the Apply button on the panel. We use this to apply the background image to a selection on the page. Figure 10.13 shows the case where the selection encompasses three words. Looking closer at the HTML code in the figure, we see that the selection on line 15 uses the <span> tags with a class attribute. This specifies the name of the CSS style which is applicable on the selection. We can view the affect of this by opening the browser, press function key F12 or File | Preview in Browser and then the respective browser (for example, iexplore). The browser output is shown in Figure 10.14.

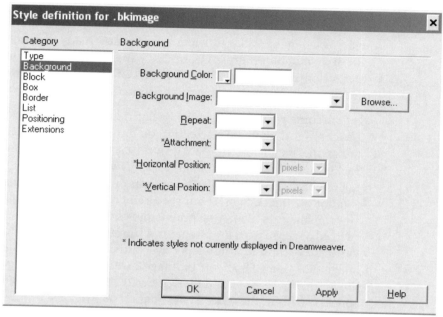

Figure 10.11 CSS style background properties panel.

We can modify attributes that belong to an existing CSS style by either using the main menu (Text | CSS Styles) or the CSS Styles panel. In addition, we can make use of the other categories that are available on the Style Definition dialogue box. For example, if we wanted a style to work with layers then we can use the Positioning category to establish desired settings.

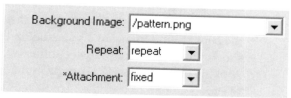

Figure 10.12 Settings for the customized style (.bkimage).

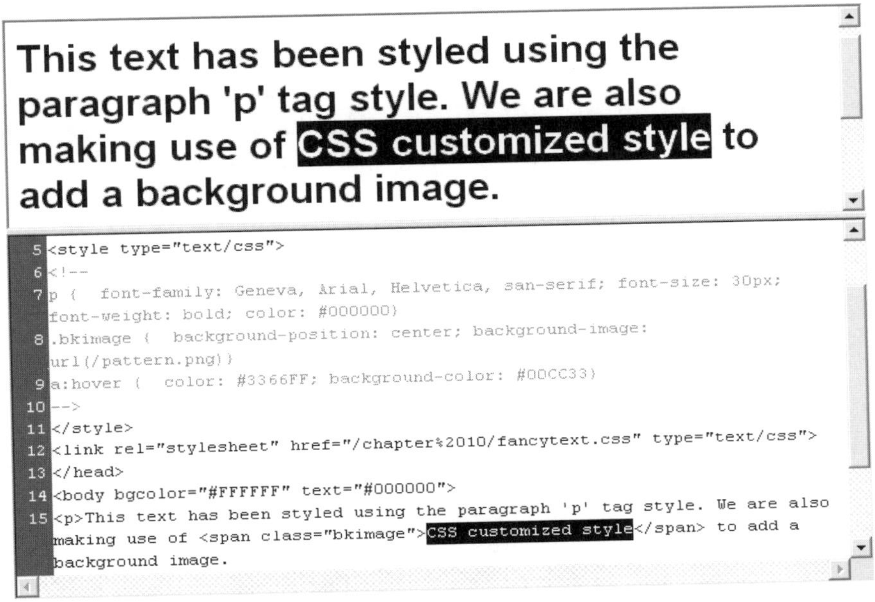

This text has been styled using the paragraph 'p' tag style. We are also making use of CSS customized style to add a background image.

```
5 <style type="text/css">
6 <!--
7 p {  font-family: Geneva, Arial, Helvetica, san-serif; font-size: 30px;
  font-weight: bold; color: #000000)
8 .bkimage {  background-position: center; background-image:
  url(/pattern.png))
9 a:hover {  color: #3366FF; background-color: #00CC33)
10 -->
11 </style>
12 <link rel="stylesheet" href="/chapter%2010/fancytext.css" type="text/css">
13 </head>
14 <body bgcolor="#FFFFFF" text="#000000">
15 <p>This text has been styled using the paragraph 'p' tag style. We are also
  making use of <span class="bkimage">CSS customized style</span> to add a
  background image.
```

Figure 10.13 Application of a CSS style on selected text.

This text has been styled using the paragraph 'p' tag style. We are also making use of CSS customized style to add a background image.

Figure 10.14 Browser display for example in Figure 10.13 (also Plate XVI).

Creating a special-effect CSS style

The third type of CSS style available is Use CSS Selector on the New Style dialogue box (opened via Text | CSS Styles, or CSS Styles panel). This provides a way of combining HTML tags, as well as offering a quick way of defining common effects, for example, mouse rollover. In the latter case, after choosing the style type, we use the Selector option to redefine the hyperlink tag, anchor <a>. As Figure 10.15 shows, we choose a:hover to realize a rollover effect. Once the OK button is pressed, the Style Definition dialogue box opens as before. We then choose a desired rollover effect. If, for example, we wanted a hyperlinked text to change colour to blue, with a green background, then we would use the Type panel for setting the blue colour and the Background panel for realizing the green colour. This rollover effect is illustrated in Figure 10.16 (also Plate XVI). The best way to understanding the workings of these categories is to experiment with them by creating a variety of styles and seeing their effect on the page.

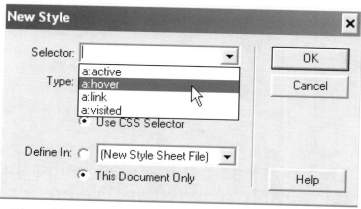

Figure 10.15 Option for creating rollover effect for hyperlinks.

Figure 10.16 Using CSS style to realize a rollover effect (also Plate XVI).

Creating an external style sheet

Thus far, we have looked at what is referred to as inline and embedded style. The styles are either defined within, for example, a paragraph or their definition resides within the head section of a page. In other words, they are applicable to the page. What commonly is required is a style sheet that can be linked to a number of pages (and sites) so that pages can be updated automatically when changes are made to a style sheet. In this case, style sheets are stored as separate files and are either referred to as linked or external style sheets. Files containing an external style sheet are given an extension of '.css' after their respective names.

We can create external style sheets from existing CSS (inline or embedded) styles by choosing any of the following ways:

- Choose File | Export and then Export CSS Styles, or
- Select Text | CSS Styles and then Export CSS Styles, or
- Use the context menu associated with the CSS Styles panel to choose Export CSS Styles.

Selecting any of these options opens the Export Styles As CSS File dialogue box. We can use this to browse to a desired folder and then to name our style sheet as required. The Dreamweaver 4.0 environment automatically creates the '.css' extension for the filename, to identify it as an external style sheet.

Alternatively, if we wanted to create a new style to be used as an external style sheet then open the New Style dialogue box (Text | CSS Styles and then New Style). This time, for the Define In option choose (New Style Sheet File). Figure 10.17 depicts the scenario.

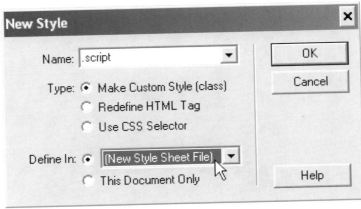

Figure 10.17 Defining an external style sheet.

Since we are defining a new external style sheet, it requires a filename. When the OK button is clicked, and as Figure 10.18 shows, the Save Style Sheet File As dialogue box opens. Enter a suitable name and then press OK. This in turn opens the Style Definition dialogue box, which (as before) allows us to define the attributes for the style. The title bar for the dialogue box this time identifies the fact that a style is being created for an external style sheet. Figure 10.19 provides an illustration of this where a style called .script is being defined for the external style sheet whose name is fancytext.

Once an external style sheet is created, it is automatically listed on the New Style dialogue panel, under Define In option (see Figure 10.17). By choosing fancytext here, for example, we can continue to add further styles to the referenced external style sheet. An icon for an external style sheet appears within the head content for a page and can be used for selection. Similarly, the CSS Styles panel shows the style with a link thumbnail to highlight the fact that it is part of an external style sheet. Figure 10.20 shows both cases, where the top image refers to the head content and the bottom image to the CSS Styles panel.

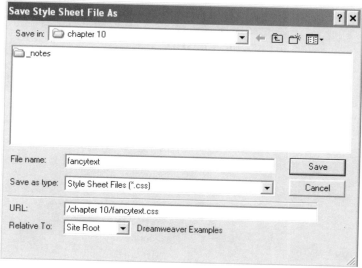

Figure 10.18 Naming a new external style sheet.

Style Definition for .script in fancytext.css

Category	Type
Type	
Background	Font:
Block	
Box	

Figure 10.19 Style Definition title bar for an external style.

Understanding forms

It is often necessary to gather information about a viewer, or their interests, or their thoughts about a product or the site itself. The most readily available way of gaining this is through a form, where the viewer makes entries to specified fields.

Forms tend to work with two components: the front end which the viewer uses to make an entry and the back end

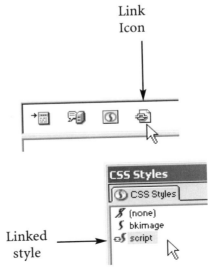

Figure 10.20 Linked style on head content and CSS Styles panel.

which takes the entry and processes it. The front end is developed using HTML code, whilst the back end involves a script (usually a CGI, Common Gateway Interface, script residing on the server side).

The Objects panel has a set of options which allow for quick inclusion of forms on a page. As Figure 10.21 shows, click on the panel's header to select the Forms category. This opens the set of options shown in Figure 10.22, where the panel settings have been changed (via Edit | Preferences and then General) to display icons and text. These options can be used to quickly add a form to a page.

Typically, a form consists of three parts: firstly, a <form> tag pair which specify the CGI script and the method which would be used to send the data to the server. Secondly, form fields which are used to get a return from the viewer. These include, for example, text fields, radio buttons, and menus. Thirdly, buttons to either submit the contents of the form to the server or to cancel.

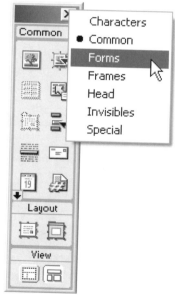

Figure 10.21 Choosing the Forms category for the Objects panel.

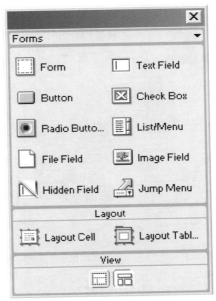

Figure 10.22 Form options on the Objects panel.

Adding a form to a page

Before, inserting a form to a page, view the preferences dialogue box and ensure that the Form Delimiter option is checked. This is located within the Invisible Elements category. Figure 10.23 depicts the scenario. Also, check to see Invisible Elements by choosing View | Visual Aids and then the corresponding option from the submenu. This, together with the Form Delimiter, allows for the display of a form outline on the page.

We start the process of adding a form by firstly placing the insertion point at a desired location on the page (where we want the form to appear). Then, we follow the steps outlined below:

● Select Insert | Form, or choose the (Insert) Form icon from the Objects panel (see Figure 10.22). As Figure 10.24

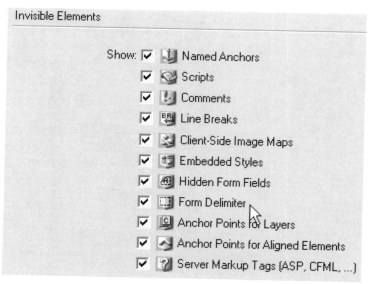

Figure 10.23 Form Delimiter option, via Preferences dialogue box.

manifests, within the design view, a rectangular box with dashed red line appears to show the form outline. The corresponding HTML tag can be seen in the code view.

- Since the tag is also selected in Figure 10.24, the Property Inspector panel displays the form attributes. Here, we can give our form a name, the method of delivery to the server, and the script to be used to process the form. The latter is specified in the text box associated with the Action option. Typically, the path for a CGI script is entered, which includes a URL to identify the server and the name of the script within the `cgi-bin` folder. An example is shown below:

```
http://www.funny.com/cgi-bin/register.cgi
```

- Having created a form description, we next add the objects to the form. If, for example, we wanted to create a text box on a page, we would use the Text Field option on the Objects panel. Clicking the option will result in a predefined sized text box appearing at the insertion point. We can also use drag and drop approach to place the text box at a different location on the page, within the form tags. Figure 10.25 depicts the scenario, where we note that the Property Inspector panel can be used to customize the text box. Use this to set the default size of the text box (via Char Width option), specify initial text for the box through Init Val, or even change the nature of the box to multiline or password.

- Next, add a label for the text box so that the viewer knows its purpose. We can achieve this by placing the insertion point either before or after the text box and then simply typing in the desired label.
- We repeat the process to insert further text boxes, as required.

In fact, the process for adding other form objects (checkboxes, menus, lists, etc) is similar to that discussed above. Each form object will have a set of attributes which are shown by the Property Inspector panel when the object is selected.

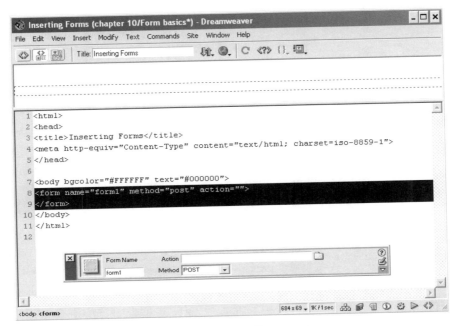

Figure 10.24 Form outline, on a page.

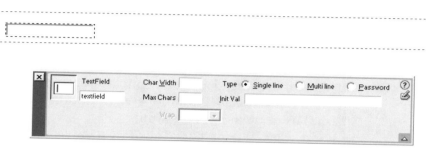

Figure 10.25 Insertion of a form text box

When entries are made via a form object, the object's identification together with its value is returned to the server. This normally is undertaken automatically, though when it comes to menus (and lists), we would need to specify the value for each item in the list. Let us look at this more closely: choose the List/Menu option from the Objects panel. As Figure 10.26 depicts, this results in a text box with an initial pull down menu arrow.

Figure 10.26 Initial state for List/Menu addition to a page.

The difference between a list and a menu is that all the list items are displayed within a text box, whilst with a menu these become available via a pull down option. The resulting Property Inspector panel is shown in Figure 10.27.

Figure 10.27 Property Inspector panel for List/Menu option.

We insert a menu list by clicking on the List Values button on the panel. This opens the corresponding dialogue box, an illustration of which is given in Figure 10.28. Here, we add the list items in the column headed Item Label. The Value column is there for us to enter the corresponding value for each item. The entry here can be the same as that for the label column. The difference between the two is their respective usage. The first column (label) is what the viewer will see, whilst the second column (value) is what is sent to the server for processing purposes. The plus and minus buttons allow for addition and removal of entries. Figure 10.29 provides an example where this has been used to create an itemized list. In the figure, the left side image shows the workings of a menu, whilst the second image depicts a list. We can use the Initially Selected option on the Property Inspector panel (see Figure 10.27) to choose the default item to be displayed. In the case of a list, use the Height option to specify the number of items to be displayed in the list window.

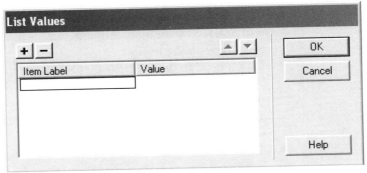

Figure 10.28 Dialogue box for creating a menu list.

Adding form buttons

Whilst text fields and menus facilitate viewer entries, we require a way of controlling form operations. These are achieved through a series of buttons. Buttons can be used to send values across to the server, clear entries in a form, and set behaviours to facilitate, for example, calculation.

Figure 10.29 Menu and List entries on a form.

We use the Button option on the Objects panel or choose `Insert | Form Objects` and then Button to add a button at the place where the insertion point is located. As shown in Figure 10.30, on the Property Inspector panel, there are the following three parameters available:

- Button Name. Type a desired name for the button, which will be used by the environment and the associated script to work with the button.
- Label. Type in desired text that will appear on top of the button. The text is for the benefit of the viewer and does not affect the behaviour or action taken by the button. The size of the button dynamically changes to fit the width of the label.
- Action. Here we set the behaviour of the button. Choose Submit, Reset or None. The latter returns a button whose behaviour can be specified through the corresponding panel. The panel is available via `Window | Behaviors` and an illustrative example is shown in Figure 10.31. We can, for example, attach a URL to the button, or add text to the status bar, or even attach a sound clip to the button. The range of options available can be found by selecting the button marked with a plus sign, on the Behaviors panel.

We can also add a graphical button to a form through using the Insert Image Field: place the insertion point within the form tags and then either select the corresponding option on the Objects panel or select `Insert | Form Objects` and then Image Field. Attach a desired image file to the field through either SRC parameter on the Property Inspector panel or the resulting Select Image Source dialogue box. We can then adjust the image attributes as required. Use function key F12 to preview the workings of the button in a browser.

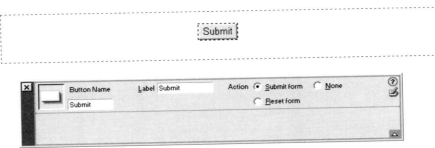

Figure 10.30 *Property Inspector panel for a (form) button.*

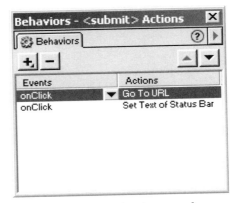

Figure 10.31 *Behaviors panel.*

Chapter 11

Testing and Publishing

Introduction

Having gone through the steps for generating the ingredients for our site, we would want finally to upload it onto a server and let the world see our production. This sounds great and, indeed, after spending some time in developing a site, we want to reach out to our target. Before we do this, however, we must make sure that the site works in the manner we expect it to. Too often, it happens that a site simply loses itself and more importantly the viewer by being unstable. Hyperlinks are not honoured and images are either broken or not found, resulting in a blank square appearing on the browser. Several rudimentary steps can be taken to ensure the site behaves in a desired fashion. The Dreamweaver 4.0 environment provides a number of ways to test, debug, manage and publish a site. The purpose of this chapter is to identify these tools so that local evaluation of the site yields returns to ensure robustness of the site functionality and usability. We will start our discussion by looking at some elementary steps which can be taken for testing a site. Some of these steps are discussed further in the subsequent sections.

Steps for site management

Typically, there are two primary problems with sites: one is that links do not work and the other is the download time is unacceptably long. Before we upload our site on to a server, we must check for these and other aspects of the site to ensure proper working. Some of the steps, which need to be addressed, are:

- Check that all external links are still valid. Sites tend to go through updates and sometimes the URL is changed to reflect the new look. Here, we can make use of a report that can be generated which checks for external links.
- Ensure that pages are displayed as expected on different browsers and that support is given for cases where a

browser may not be able to display an element. The support may simply be in the form of a text message covering information about the missing element. We can also use the Dreamweaver 4.0 environment to switch pages depending upon the browser being used.

- Monitor download times for pages. Images and tables included on a page, for example, will take time to download. We need to check the download time to ensure that this meets our requirements. The environment can be used to assess this for different bandwidth settings.
- We can generate a number of reports to test and evaluate the complete site. This can be used to identify problems with nested or empty tags, for example.
- Test JavaScript code to ensure that it executes as expected. Use the on-board debugger to check and rectify any errors.

We will look at these aspects in greater detail and especially how the environment can assist us in the following sections.

Managing links

We are already familiar with the fact that linked items, within a site, are automatically updated if they are moved to another folder or are renamed. The environment, in fact, prompts to confirm that we actually do wish to update the link. Figure 11.1 gives an illustrative example of the Update Files message box. We can select and update individual files, if the list contains more than one file.

Links usually can be checked manually, but as the site develops, it becomes tedious (if not impossible) to keep track of all links. Large organizations provide a number of services and having a site to cover them would require many links, both internal and external to the site.

The Dreamweaver 4.0 environment has a Check Links feature which tracks internal links and makes a list of all external references (but these are not verified). The Check Links option looks for three types of links: broken, external and

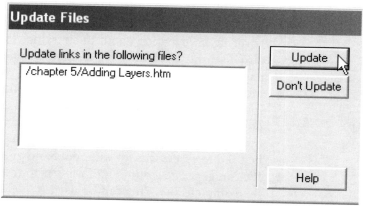

Figure 11.1 Message prompt for updating a link.

orphaned. To check a page, choose File | Check Links. To verify links for part of a site, do the following:

● Open the Site window by choosing Window | Site Files.
● Within the Local Folder view, select the files and folders to be checked.
● Then choose File | Check Links (on the Site window) to begin the process.

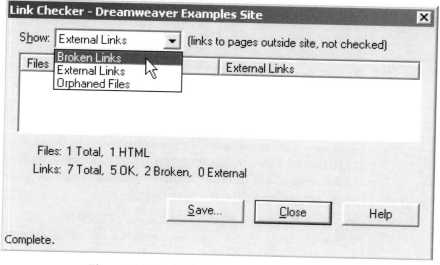

Figure 11.2 Link Checker (report) dialogue box.

● The Link Checker dialogue box then opens with a report. As Figure 11.2 depicts, we can choose by using the Show parameter to view broken links, external links, or orphaned files. The total number of links, together with the number of broken and external are also listed. If, for example, we chose to view broken links then we would see two such links. By clicking on the link within the Broken Links column, a folder appears which facilitates rectification of the problem by entering a workable link. Figure 11.3 provides an illustration of this scenario.

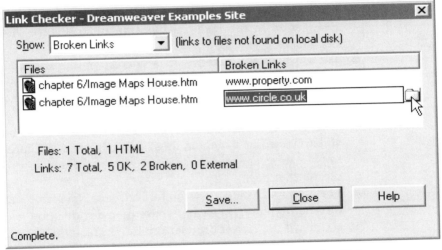

Figure 11.3 An approach for rectifying a broken link.

In addition, to check all links belonging to a site, select Site | Check Links Sitewide. The Link Checker dialogue box opens containing a report for all the links appearing on the site. In this case, we also have access to links that have been orphaned. In other words, those files that exist on the site, but are no longer linked. All reports can be stored for future reference by using the Save option on the Link Checker dialogue box.

Changing browsers

We can use the Dreamweaver 4.0 environment to load different pages depending upon the viewer's browser type and version. The purpose of this is to ensure that the site is presentable irrespective of the browser being used. We use the Check Browser action to set this up. The first step in achieving this is to select an object from the page and then do the following:

- Choose `Window | Behaviors` to open the Behaviors panel.
- Click on the plus signed button and choose Check Browser from the resulting pop-up menu. Figure 11.4 depicts the scenario.
- We are then presented with a corresponding dialogue box, an illustration of which is shown in Figure 11.5. We can choose a variety of options depending upon how we want the page to be viewed. For example, do we want everyone with a version of browser greater than 3.0 to be able to view this page? Or, those using Internet Explorer to view this page and those using Netscape Navigator to see another page.
- Through specifying a version for Netscape Navigator and Internet Explorer, in each case we then decide upon two actions: if the viewer browser version is greater than one, do action, otherwise do another action.
- The action in each case is shown in Figure 11.6 and can be summarized as follows:
  - ○ Go to URL. Jump to the desired web address.
  - ○ Go to Alt URL. Jump to a different web address.
  - ○ Stay on the Page. Do nothing, just display current page.
- Other browsers may include text-based (such as Lynx) and the option for these should also be chosen. It is probably best to stick with Stay on This Page as the choice here.
- Specify the filenames for (Go to) URL and (Go to) Alt URL.
- Press OK to activate the attributes.

Figure 11.4 Check Browser option on Behaviors panel.

In addition, the Check Plugin action can be used to load different pages depending upon whether a browser has a specified plugin. This is also available via the Behaviors panel.

Viewing download performance

An estimate of the download time for the current page is given within the launcher bar. Figure 11.7 depicts the scenario, where the size of the file covers all elements, including linked objects.

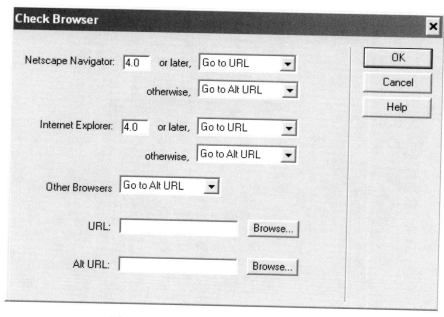

Figure 11.5   *Check Browser dialogue box.*

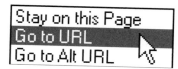

Figure 11.6   *Page display options for a browser.*

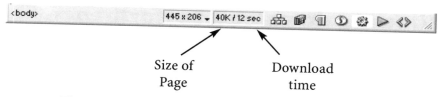

Size of   Download
Page   time

Figure 11.7   *Page size and download time, on launcher bar.*

The Dreamweaver 4.0 environment estimates the download time by using the connection speed specified in the preferences dialogue box. Within this, choose the Status Bar category and then use the Connection Speed parameter to choose a value for this. Figure 11.8 gives an illustration of the available connection speeds supported by the environment.

It is best to experiment with different connection speeds to see how this affects the download times. The download times returned by the environment are meant to be indicative rather than actual, since much will depend on the traffic on the Internet when the page is downloaded. We should, clearly, aim for fast downloads and, typically, this means that a page needs to download completely within ten seconds of the request being made. Set an average connection speed, say, 28.8 or 33.6 kbs during development, as this would provide a good indication of how the page will load when published.

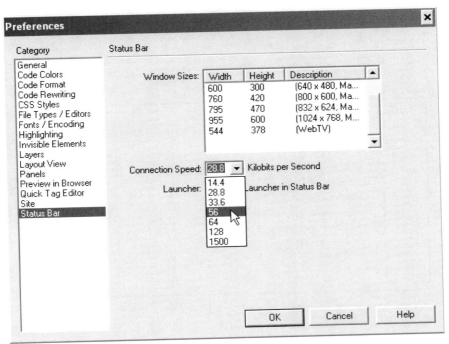

Figure 11.8 *Establishing a connection speed for downloads.*

Generating reports

A key feature of Dreamweaver 4.0 is that it can generate (feedback) reports about a site. This provides useful information about the files, folders and any troubleshooting aspects that require further action. The latter centres around HTML tags, where nested font tags, missing Alt text, redundant nested tags, removable empty tags and untitled documents, as well as external links are checked. We have the choice of specifying the scope for the check. Choose current document, entire site, selected files, or a desired folder. In addition, the report results can be filtered and further information on selected results can be sought.

To open the report dialogue box, choose Site | Reports. The corresponding dialogue box is shown in Figure 11.9. The

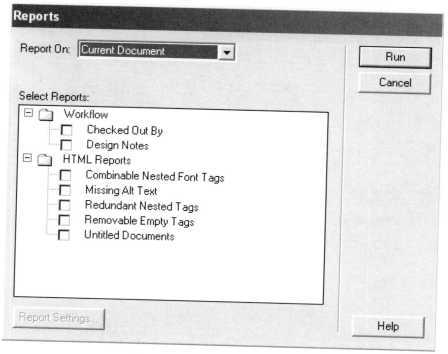

Figure 11.9 Reports dialogue box.

Report On option allows us to set the scope of the check. In the figure shown, we are then presented with two types of reports, one for the workflow and the other focusing on HTML tags. In the case of the former, this supports team working, where some collaboration has taken place to develop a site. The two options associated with workflow identify who has checked the files and whether any design notes are available. Clicking on either option activates the Report Settings button (located at bottom left of the dialogue box). This, in general, is used to seek further information about the chosen option. For example, selecting Checked Out By opens the text box shown in Figure 11.10, where a team member's details can be entered. By choosing Design Notes, we can customize the report to include files with design notes that contain desired keywords. Figure 11.11 shows the settings for this, where a comparison pull down menu (middle option) can be used to establish the nature of the report.

Figure 11.10 Text box for Checked Out By option.

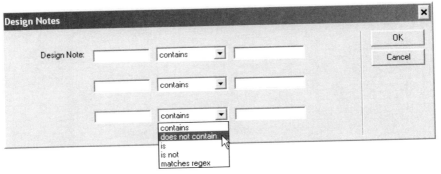

Figure 11.11 Settings for customizing design notes report.

The second type of reports is centred on HTML codes. We can check any of the items listed in the Reports dialogue box. If, for example, we wanted to identify any cases of redundant nested tags in the entire site, we would select the corresponding report checkbox on the dialogue box (see Figure 11.9).

To generate a report, we click on the Run button on the Reports dialogue box. The environment then goes about checking files and folders that are within the specified range. Any corrective action which maybe required whilst checking is in progress is highlighted through a system prompt. This, for example, could be identification of invalid HTML tags.

A Results window opens once the checking is completed. Figure 11.12 gives an illustrative example. The report, as depicted by the figure, gives a listing of problem areas. We can order the list in terms of the column headings. For example, if we wanted to have the results in terms of problem areas, we would click on the column header labelled 'Description'.

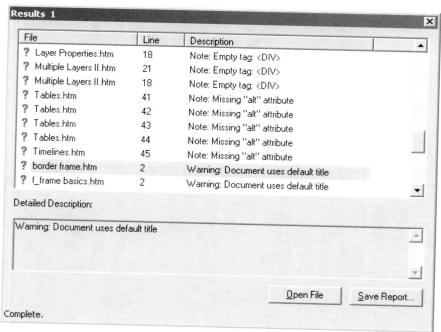

Figure 11.12 Results window showing outcome of desired checks.

Additional details, if any, about the problem are provided in the Detailed Description section of the Results window. We can view and rectify the problem by either selecting and using Open File button, or double-clicking a result row. This opens the document window with the problem highlighted. Figure 11.13 shows an example, where for an image, the alternative (Alt) text is missing. The file identified with this omission is Tables.htm and the error is on line 42 of the source code. The <img> tag is also highlighted to quickly see the problem area.

Clicking on the Save Report button stores the contents of the Results window. The report is saved as an XML file, which can be imported into a spreadsheet or database for printing purposes, or viewed within a browser.

We can use an option on the main menu to clean up some of the errors in the HTML coding: choose Commands | Clean Up HTML to invoke the dialogue box shown in Figure 11.14. We can choose to remove certain tags (for example, empty tags, redundant tags, etc) and specific tags (such as those included by a visual editor). Additional options include combining nested <font> tags. This tracks the case where

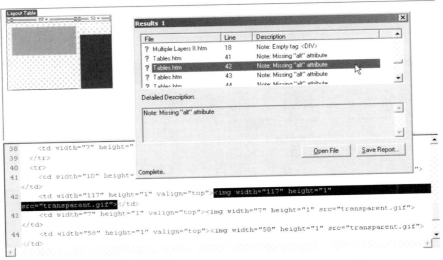

Figure 11.13 Using Results window to open a listed file.

the font tag is used twice, for example, to specify attributes. The option will combine the two into a single tag with two attributes. The second option is for producing a message at the end of the process, highlighting what has been cleaned up. Figure 11.15 depicts an example.

Debugging JavaScript

The Dreamweaver 4.0 environment features a debugger that can be used to locate both syntax and logical errors. Syntax errors prompt a browser message, whilst logical errors, which are not reported by a browser, result in the script returning a different result than that which it was designed for. As with most, if not all, debugger programs, we can set breakpoints at desired locations to inspect values of variables and run a script incrementally so that variables can be viewed at every step of the code.

We can run the debugger by either choosing File | Debug in Browser and then select a browser (for example, iexplore for Internet Explorer), or making use of the browser button on the toolbar and clicking on the Debug in iexplore option. Figure 11.16 depicts the scenario.

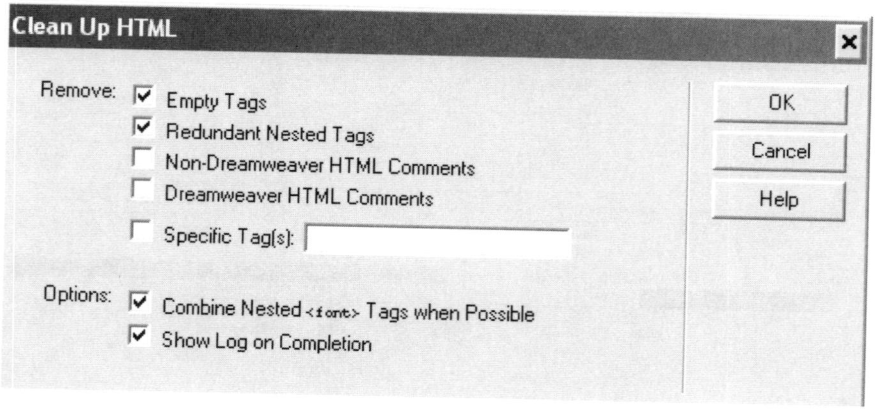

Figure 11.14 Clean Up HTML dialogue box.

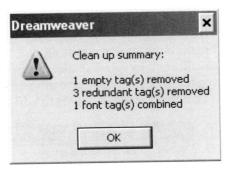

Figure 11.15 Log message box showing clean up operations.

Before the debugger opens, a Java security message prompt appears. Simply choose the Yes button to allow the debugger to communicate with the browser. No network connection (for example to an Internet server) is actually made.

The JavaScript debugger should then open. As Figure 11.17 highlights, it is split into two sections: the top window displays the code and, for example, the breakpoints. The bottom window gives a list of variables and their respective values (up to any set breakpoint).

The buttons on the header provide the control for the debugger. With reference to Figure 11.18, these are sectionalized into three: the left two buttons start and stop the debugging process; the middle two buttons set and clear breakpoints; and the right side three buttons allow for step increments.

When the debugger is run, it checks for syntax errors first. If it finds an error then it displays a dialogue box similar to that shown in Figure 11.19. If we click on the Go to Line button,

Figure 11.16 Invoking the debugger via the toolbar.

the environment highlights the line where the error resides. Logical errors are then located through using the breakpoints and examining the variables. We can add a breakpoint by placing the insertion point within a code (statement) line and then choosing Add breakpoint button. The button acts as a toggle to add and remove a breakpoint.

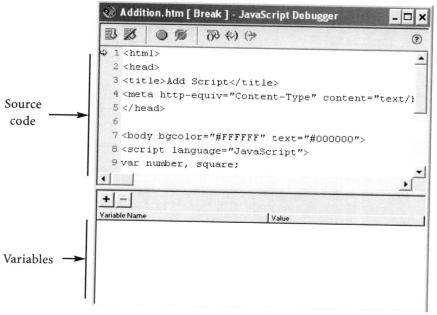

Source code

Variables

Figure 11.17 Debugger window.

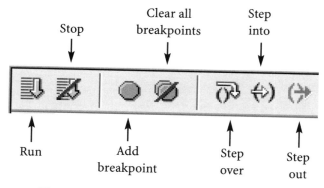

Figure 11.18 Control buttons for the debugger.

In addition, we can use the three buttons on the right side of the header to fine-tune the debugging through manually stepping through (or over) the code and noting the values in the variable. This usually happens, in practice, after a breakpoint has been reached for a given script.

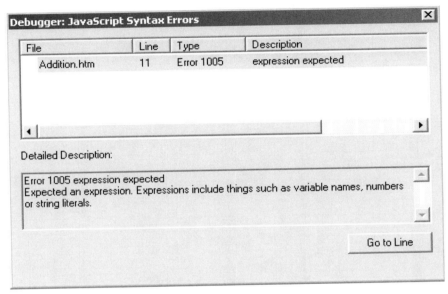

Figure 11.19 JavaScript Syntax Errors window.

Publishing a site

Having worked hard to design and develop a site, we would want others, especially our audience, to be able to both view and use the components on the site. In order for this to be realized, we must move (or copy) our site to a (web) server, which in turn allows users to access the necessary files. The server may reside locally within an organization or be accessible remotely through the Internet. Either way, we must transfer our files to a server to publish the site.

Within the Dreamweaver 4.0 environment, we need to supply (what is referred to as) remote information to get a local site published. The necessary steps are as follows:

- Choose Site | Define Sites to open the corresponding dialogue box.
- Select an existing site and click on the Edit button. This opens the Site Definition dialogue box.
- Choose Remote Info as the category. The dialogue box should then look similar to that shown in Figure 11.20 (for a site titled Dreamweaver Examples).

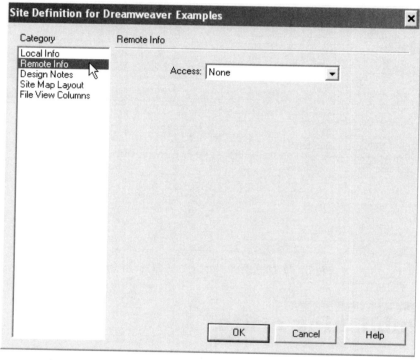

Figure 11.20 Remote Info category, on Site definition window.

- Click on the pull-down menu for the Access parameter to reveal the options shown in Figure 11.21.
- If we wanted to load the site to a local web sever which is accessible through LAN, then click on the Local/Network option. This will update the dialogue box to that shown in Figure 11.22. Then, do the following:
  - For Remote Folder parameter, enter path to the local web server or use the folder icon to locate the folder on the network.

- ○ Check the Refresh option if the remote site is to be updated automatically. Otherwise, leave it unchecked and manually update the remote site to improve system performance.
- ○ If collaborating, identify the person who can check out the files by entering their name in the text box labelled Check Out Name and type in a convenient email address. Otherwise, leave the Check In/Out box unchecked.

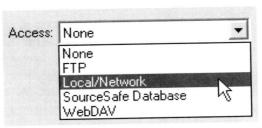

Figure 11.21 Server access options for remote site.

- To upload the site to a remote web server, choose FTP as the option for the Access parameter. This results in the dialogue box offering the options shown in Figure 11.23. Then, do the following:

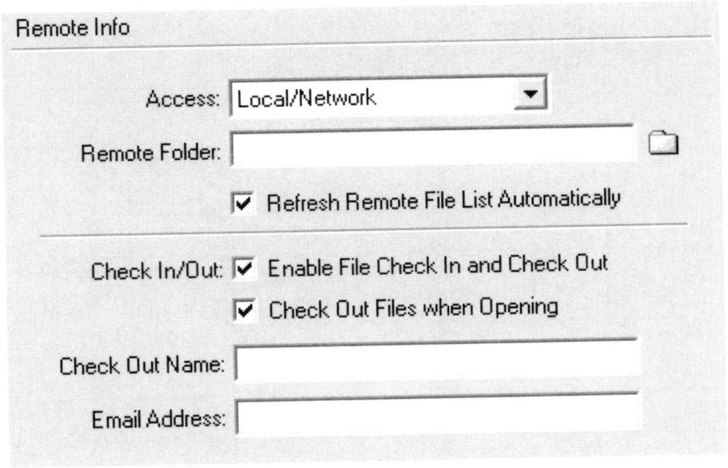

Remote Info

Access: Local/Network

Remote Folder:

☑ Refresh Remote File List Automatically

Check In/Out: ☑ Enable File Check In and Check Out

☑ Check Out Files when Opening

Check Out Name:

Email Address:

Figure 11.22 Options for local delivery of site.

- ○ For FTP Host, enter the name of the FTP server. For example: ftp.luqman.com.

○ For Host Directory, enter the root folder for the web site. This should reflect the local root folder to ensure that links (and therefore the site) work properly.

○ For Login and Password, type in the normal values when accessing the remote web server. By default, the password is saved. Deselect Save checkbox to receive a prompt each time access to the remote site is required.

○ Use Passive FTP and Use Firewall options should be set after checking with whoever is looking after the organizations networks, in particular access to the Intranet and Internet. This may result in configuring further the FTP and firewall settings through the preferences dialogue box. Choose `Edit | Preferences` and then Site as the category to view and edit the respective options.

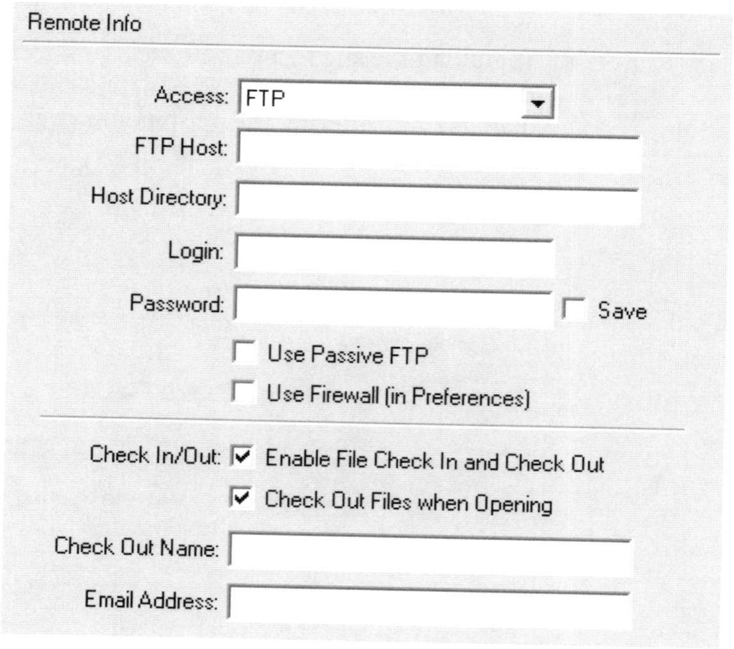

```
Remote Info

             Access: [FTP                    ▼]
           FTP Host: [                        ]
     Host Directory: [                        ]
             Login:  [                        ]
          Password:  [                        ]   □ Save
                     □ Use Passive FTP
                     □ Use Firewall (in Preferences)

      Check In/Out: ☑ Enable File Check In and Check Out
                    ☑ Check Out Files when Opening
    Check Out Name: [                        ]
     Email Address: [                        ]
```

Figure 11.23 *Options for remote web server, via FTP.*

Index